2440

*Critical Elections
and the Mainsprings of
American Politics*

Critical Elections

and the Mainsprings of American Politics

WALTER DEAN BURNHAM

WASHINGTON UNIVERSITY

W · W · NORTON & COMPANY · INC · NEW YORK

For Tish

Contents

Preface

The study of American electoral politics is, like the subject itself, studded with paradoxes. It is old and yet young; it is at once sophisticated and naïve. We have acquired an enormous range of information about the individual American voter and the social-psychological factors which shape his political consciousness and actions, yet there remain a great many lacunae in our understanding of American politics. They appear to be particularly concentrated at the level of macroanalysis, where the concern is with the quantitative study of an aggregate system of behavior rather than with the behavior of individuals within that system.

The reasons for the persistence of these lacunae are both complex and numerous, but two seem to have been of particular importance. The first is what might be described as technological. The enormous universe of elective offices in the United States has provided one set of limits on the use of aggregate data, as has the extraordinary diversity in the quality of the states' reporting of elections and in their accessibility to scholars in usable form. Erwin Scheuch has admirably discussed the comparative implications of this aspect of American disaggregation: it casts light on the nature of this political system.[1] It is only too clear that in such a context the construction and subsequent analysis of national, stratified samples of the American electorate would be most

[1] Erwin Scheuch, "Cross-National Comparisons Using Aggregate Data," in Stein Rokkan and Richard Merritt (eds.), *Comparing Nations* (New Haven: Yale University Press, 1966), pp. 131–68.

useful to scholars in solving this problem.

The second limiting condition has been cultural. This aspect of our political knowledge and its limitations are discussed more extensively in the concluding part of this work, and it is enough to note two points of significance here. The first is that, as Richard Jensen has recently pointed out, the behavioral revolution in political science drew very heavily from psychology in its early stages, rather than from sociology, economics, or history.[2] The psychological tradition has remained particularly strong in the study of voting behavior, since an emphasis on survey methods has carried with it an emphasis on the individual's motivational basis for the political choices he makes. One cannot say how much of this was due to historical accident—for example, to the availability of relevant individuals and techniques at the time when Charles Merriam organized his conferences at the University of Chicago in the mid-1920's—but it can be suggested that the necessarily short time span of survey analysis has until quite recently entailed a rather episodic, snapshot view of the American voter and the system in which he functions. Longitudinal analysis of such materials has had to wait until the 1960's—that is, until there was both a time series of some length and a diversity of election situations great enough to qualify the premature generalizations about voting behavior which were found in the earlier literature.

But in addition to this, the mainstream of quantitative-behavioral research on American politics has until very recently been peculiarly insensitive to the time dimension. This is faithfully reflected in the basic textbooks through which students are introduced to the field, in which they learn of the extreme stability and durability, the givenness, of our political institutions—including the political parties—and the

[2] Richard Jensen, "History and the Political Scientist," in Seymour M. Lipset (ed.), *Politics and the Social Sciences* (New York: Oxford University Press, 1969), pp. 1–28.

dominance of such elements as bargaining, political consensus, and incremental, gradual adjustments in the policy process. There is no doubt that our institutions *have* been immensely durable and that bargaining and incrementalism help to define the liberal pluralism we all know. Yet this is not the whole story by any means, and the timelessness of the American political-science mainstream represents a major conceptual problem. It is not for this work to unravel that problem in any detail; it can only be suggested here that the "irrational liberalism" which Louis Hartz has defined as our master set of political values tends to be oblivious, if not actually hostile, to the kind of historical awareness which informed the consciousness of the giants of classical European sociology.

But as America has at length merged with the rest of the world during the past generation, the hold of this master set of values has clearly been weakened. American political science has also been caught up in the ferment of change. One aspect of this has been that ecological-systemic analysis of voting behavior with an explicit time dimension has become much more frequently employed. Such analysis can be seen, for example, in the more recent work of the Survey Research Center and of a political geographer, Kevin Cox. It combines concern for systemic questions which have hitherto been the focus of macroanalysis with thorough sophistication in the use of quantitative methodology. Bridges are being built between one level of analysis and another, and the late V. O. Key, Jr., has become a less isolated figure than he once was.

Such work cannot but contribute to a long-overdue reorganization of the ways in which we think about the American political system. Similarly, the construction of a massive, computerized data archive of political and ecological information at the Inter-University Consortium for Political Research has at last given us a technological breakthrough which can only stimulate longitudinal analysis and, consequently, the growth of a sense of history in the study of voting behavior. The present study constitutes a modest and very preliminary use of some of the riches of this data. It will also contribute, it is hoped, to a rethinking of the processes of American politics and of the place of quantitative history in the flow of these processes across time.

A few conventional observations should be made about this study. It constitutes a part of a much larger effort to analyze aggregate electoral behavior in the United States in historical depth. Indeed, it should be regarded as the first of a series of studies of the dynamic movements which are so central to the past and present pattern of American politics. Such studies should serve to refine, elaborate, qualify, and—possibly—refute many of the hypotheses advanced here concerning these movements and their implications.

This work and the larger project on which it is based in its quantitative aspects have been supported by the National Science Foundation under Grant GS-2272.

My appreciation goes to my graduate assistants, Karl T. Kurtz and Daniel Mazmanian; both their labor in acquiring and processing data and their comments on this work have been helpful to me. I should also like in particular to thank Professors Gerald M. Pomper and Robert H. Salisbury for their informative comments on and criticisms of this work in an earlier version. It goes without saying that the responsibility for any errors of fact or deficiencies of analysis is mine alone. In particular, it should be stressed that the views expressed in this study are in no way to be ascribed to the National Science Foundation or any of its personnel.

It is usual for an author to acknowledge that his concentrated labor on a book has cost his family a good deal: the twenty-four-hour day binds us all. I can only add my own gratitude here for my wife's forbearance, moral support, and critical assistance.

*Critical Elections
and the Mainsprings of
American Politics*

1

Toward a Definition of Critical Realignment

For many decades it has been generally recognized that American electoral politics is not quite "all of a piece" despite its apparent diverse uniformity. Some elections have more important long-range consequences for the political system as a whole than others, and seem to "decide" substantive issues in a more clear-cut way. There has long been agreement among historians that the elections of those of 1800, 1828, 1860, 1896, and 1932, for example, were fundamental turning points in the course of American electoral politics.

Since the appearance in 1955 of V. O. Key's seminal article, "A Theory of Critical Elections," political scientists have moved to give this concept quantitative depth and meaning. In his article, Key isolated New England data in order to demonstrate the differential impact of a compressing sectionalism in the 1890's and of a class-ethnic polarity which emerged in the

1

1928–36 period.[1] Duncan MacRae Jr. and James A. Meldrum, in 1960, employed the sophistications of factor analysis applied to residuals to isolate realigning cycles from short-term deviation in Illinois, a discriminant technique that, surprisingly, has been little used in subsequent articles on American voting behavior. They concluded that it is usually more appropriate to conceptualize critical realignments as involving a closely spaced but massive series of adjustments in the mass base than as single events.[2]

In the same year the authors of *The American Voter* developed a typology of elections which included realigning elections—although, of course, on the basis of historical evidence rather than on grounds then observable in survey-research data.[3] Also writing in 1960, E. E. Schattschneider—employing little data but fertile insight—addressed our attention to the utility of viewing the structure of politics brought into being by realignments as systems of action: in the aftermath of realignment, not only voting behavior but institutional roles and policy outputs undergo substantial modifications.[4]

Work done by a number of scholars during the 1960's has fleshed out our empirical knowledge of some of the processes associated with critical realignment. For example, evidence has been brought forward that the adjustments of the 1890's were accompanied and followed by significant transformations in the rules of the game and in the behavioral properties of the American electorate. It has also been suggested that each era between realignments can be described as having its own

[1] V. O. Key, Jr., "A Theory of Critical Elections," 17 *Journal of Politics*, pp. 3–18 (1955).

[2] Duncan MacRae, Jr., and James A. Meldrum, "Critical Elections in Illinois: 1888–1958," 54 *American Political Science Review*, pp. 669–83 (1960).

[3] Angus Campbell *et al.*, *The American Voter* (New York: Wiley & Sons, 1960), pp. 531–38.

[4] E. E. Schattschneider, *The Semisovereign People* (New York: Holt, Rinehart & Winston, 1960), especially pp. 78–96.

"party system," even if the formal names of the major parties which form most of its organizational base happen to remain unchanged. A Schattschneiderian analysis has very recently been applied to California for the 1890–1910 period and found to work quite well.[5]

At the same time, there has been rather little effort directed to the task of exploring these phenomena in terms of their implications for effective analysis of American politics across time and space. While Key entitled his seminal article "A *Theory* of Critical Elections," and while both he and Schattschneider clearly regarded realignments of fundamental analytical importance, one is impressed with how little theorizing has been forthcoming in this area. One reason for this paucity may well be an annoying incompleteness in certain key ranges of data analysis; this often leaves us in controversy not only as to the implications of the facts of change, but even as to the structure of those facts themselves.[6]

It now seems time to attempt at least an interim assessment of the structure, function, and implications of critical realignments for the American political process. Such an effort is motivated in particular by the author's view that critical realignments are of fundamental importance not only to the system of political action called "the American political process" but also to the clarifications of some aspects of its operation. It seems particularly important in a period of obvious political upheaval not only to identify these phenomena and place them in time, but to integrate them into a larger (if still very modest) theory of movement in American politics.

Such a theory must inevitably emphasize the elements of

[5] Michael Rogin, "California Populism and the 'System of 1896,'" 22 *Western Political Quarterly*, pp. 179–96 (1969).

[6] Such seems more than implicit, for instance, in the arguments made recently by H. D. Price; see his contribution to Oliver Garceau (ed.), *Political Research and Political Theory* (Cambridge: Harvard University Press, 1968), especially pp. 115–20.

stress and abrupt transformation in our political life at the expense of the consensual, gradualist perspectives which have until recently dominated the scholar's vision of American political processes and behavior. For the realignment phenomenon focuses our attention on "the dark side of the moon." It reminds us that politics as usual in the United States is not politics as always; that there are discrete types of voting behavior and quite different levels of voter response to political stimuli, depending on what those stimuli are and at what point in time they occur; and that American political institutions and leadership, once defined (or redefined) in a "normal phase" of our politics, seem to become part of the very conditions that threaten to overthrow them.

The work of survey research over the past generation has heavily confirmed what earlier students and practitioners of politics in the United States noted: once a stable pattern of voting behavior and of generalized leadership recruitment has been established, it tends to continue over time with only short-term deviations. As is well known, for example, party identification in the 1952–64 period showed only the most glacial movement, in sharp contrast to the actual partisan outcomes of elections. When differentials in turnout among population groups are taken into account, it is possible to derive both a "normal vote" and a normal majority party—about 52 to 53 per cent Democratic for the country as a whole in recent years.[7] Short-term deviations occur, of course, and have been showing a marked tendency to increase since the 1940's. But the dominant structure of party-oriented voting, which comes out more clearly in the aggregate totals for Congress than in presidential elections, has remained highly fixed until very recently. Thus recent presidential and congressional elections present the national profile shown in Table 1.1.

---

[7] See Philip E. Converse, "The Concept of a Normal Vote," in Angus Campbell *et al.*, *Elections and the Political Order* (New York: Wiley & Sons, 1968), pp. 9–39.

Table 1.1 National Presidential and Congressional
Elections, 1944–1968

	Presidential	*Congressional*
% Democratic of total vote	49.0	52.1
Variance	45.65	8.05
Standard Deviation	6.76	2.84
% Republican of total vote	47.9	46.6
Variance	43.94	6.31
Standard Deviation	6.63	2.51
% Democratic of two-party vote	50.6	52.8
Variance	39.30	7.14
Standard Deviation	6.27	2.67

Stable phases in the alignment cycle are not identical, of course, with complete uniformity of behavior. Not only are deviating elections such as 1952 or 1956 possible, but also secular trends within regions or discrete groupings of voters and even fairly major but localized readjustments—for example, the emergence and flourishing of presidential Republicanism in the South during the Eisenhower era. Such movements can be of considerable long-term political significance in their own right. For example, between the 1930's and the mid-1960's there was a trend toward secular realignment in favor of the Democrats in much of the Northeast, and in favor of the Republicans in border and midwestern states such as Kentucky and Illinois.[8] Indeed, one of the aspects of the contemporary political scene which we shall examine at some length is the increasing instability of major sectors of the mass electorate.[9] Since this trend in no small way acts as a limiting

[8] John H. Fenton, *Midwest Politics* (New York: Holt, Rinehart & Winston, 1966), pp. 214–18; and, by the same author, *Politics in the Border States* (New Orleans: Hauser, 1957), pp. 114–17.
[9] American party alignments since World War II have shown very high lability compared with those of most other Western polities. See Richard Rose and Derek Urwin, "Persistence and Change in Western

condition on nationwide realignment in the current era, it is of the greatest importance for the analysis of contemporary electoral politics in this country.

It is enough to say for the present that any working definition of the concept "critical realignment" must, practically speaking, eliminate both deviating election situations— even landslides such as Theodore Roosevelt's in 1904 or Warren Harding's in 1920—and gradual secular realignments. It must also emphasize that while there are large historical, territorial, and stratification differences in the stability of "stable phases," they reveal comparatively far more of a component of political inertia at the mass base than do realigning eras.

In its "ideal-typical" form, the critical realignment differs from stable alignments eras, secular realignments, and deviating elections in the following basic ways.

1. The critical realignment is characteristically associated with short-lived but very intense disruptions of traditional patterns of voting behavior. Majority parties become minorities; politics which was once competitive becomes noncompetitive or, alternatively, hitherto one-party areas now become arenas of intense partisan competition; and large blocks of the active electorate—minorities, to be sure, but perhaps involving as much as a fifth to a third of the voters—shift their partisan allegiance.

2. Critical elections are characterized by abnormally high intensity as well.

a. This intensity typically spills over into the party nominat-

Party Systems Since 1945," (Cologne: Conference on Comparative Social Science, 26–31 May 1969, mimeo), especially Table 7B following p. 17. The only set of parties which show a larger standard deviation of vote change over this period are the Gaullist and MRP parties in France, and the reason in that case is obvious. Standard deviations of magnitudes comparable with those for the two American parties are also found for the two major Canadian parties (not surprisingly) and for the German CDU/CSU. No other major parties in the nineteen countries studied reveal standard deviations which are nearly so large.

ing and platform-writing machinery during the upheaval and results in major shifts in convention behavior from the integrative "norm" as well as in transformations in the internal loci of power in the major party most heavily affected by the pressures of realignment. Ordinarily accepted "rules of the game" are flouted; the party's processes, instead of performing their usual integrative functions, themselves contribute to polarization.

b. The rise in intensity is associated with a considerable increase in ideological polarizations, at first within one or more of the major parties and then between them. Issue distances between the parties are markedly increased, and elections tend to involve highy salient issue-clusters, often with strongly emotional and symbolic overtones, far more than is customary in American electoral politics. One curious property of established leadership as it drifts into the stress of realignment seems to be a tendency to become more rigid and dogmatic, which itself contributes greatly to the explosive "bursting stress" of realignment. Federalist leadership just before 1801 stands in marked contrast to the Jeffersonian afterward, for example. The same may be said (perhaps less certainly) of the inherited inner-circle political style of a John Quincy Adams as the antideferential democratic revolution got under way; of the inflexible leadership of a James Buchanan in 1857–61, which effectively foreclosed a middle-of-the-road northern Democratic alternative to the Republicans; of the rigid defense of the status quo waged by Grover Cleveland and Herbert Hoover in our two greatest depressions; and of Lyndon Johnson's unhappy second administration.[10]

c. The rise in intensity is also normally to be found in abnor-

---

[10] Certainly this generational collision was of very great prominence in the 1968 Democratic convention at Chicago. For an excellent delegate's-eye view of this, see Aaron Wildavsky, "The Meaning of 'Youth' in the Struggle for Control of the Democratic Party" (mimeo).

mally heavy voter participation for the time. This significant increase in political mobilization is not always or uniformly present, to be sure. It is particularly true of realigning cycles with a strong sectional thrust that the areas which are propelled most strongly to one party or the other tend to be those in which turnout does not increase much, or even declines. Similarly, while increases in participation during the 1928–36 period were very heavy in most of the country, they were slight or nonexistent in the South, because the restrictive structure of local politics which had been created at the turn of the century was not disturbed until long after World War II. Moreover, the net effect of the New Deal realignment was to make the South even more lopsidedly Democratic than it had been before. With such exceptions, however, there has still been a general tendency toward markedly increased participation during realigning eras.

3. Historically speaking, at least, national critical realignments have not occurred at random. Instead, there has been a remarkably uniform periodicity in their appearance. A variety of measures can be employed to examine this periodic phenomenon. Sudden shifts in the relationship between percentages for a given political party in one election and the next can be easily detected through autocorrelation and may present strong evidence of realignment.[11] Another technique, analogous to discriminant-function or change-in-universe-state analysis, will be discussed later. Here it is sufficient to assert that this periodicity has had an objective existence, that it is one of the most striking historically conditioned facts associated with the evolution of American electoral politics, and that it is of very great analytical importance.

[11] Gerald Pomper, "Classification of Presidential Elections," 29 *Journal of Politics*, pp. 535–66 (1967); and Walter Dean Burnham, "American Voting Behavior and the 1964 Election," 12 *Midwest Journal of Political Science*, pp. 1–40 (1968).

4. It has been argued, with much truth, that American political parties are essentially constituent parties.[12] That is to say, the political-party subsystem is sited in a socioeconomic system of very great heterogeneity and diversity. For a variety of reasons (to be discussed in greater detail later) this party system has tended to be preoccupied with performing the functions of integration and "automatic" aggregation of highly diverse and often antagonistic subgroupings in the population to the near exclusion of concern for development of "modern" mass organization in the European sense. It is neither structured nor widely perceived as a cohesive policy link between voters and officials. The conditions in which our political parties operate, and their normal operating styles and limitations, have produced not a little anguish among an older generation of political scientists who grew to professional maturity during the New Deal and who rightly saw the structure and functioning of our major political parties as a major obstacle to the realization of democratic accountability.[13] It has been well said that "electorally, American parties represent outcomes *in general;* parties seldom shape or represent outcomes *in particular.*"[14]

Critical realignments emerge directly from the dynamics of this constituent-function supremacy in American politics in ways and with implications which will be analyzed subsequently. Here we will only note that since they involve constitutional readjustments in the broadest sense of the term, they are intimately associated with and followed by transformations in large clusters of policy. This produces correspond-

[12] Theodore J. Lowi, "Party, Policy, and Constitution" in William N. Chambers and Walter Dean Burnham (eds.), *The American Party Systems* (New York: Oxford University Press, 1967), pp. 238–76.

[13] The *locus classicus* here is, of course, the report of the APSA's Committee on Political Parties, *Toward a More Responsible Two-Party System* (1950).

[14] Lowi, *op. cit.,* p. 263.

ingly profound alternations in policy and influences the grand institutional structures of American government. In other words, realignments are themselves constituent acts: they arise from emergent tensions in society which, not adequately controlled by the organization or outputs of party politics as usual, escalate to a flash point; they are issue-oriented phenomena, centrally associated with these tensions and more or less leading to resolution adjustments; they result in significant transformations in the general shape of policy; and they have relatively profound aftereffects on the roles played by institutional elites.[15] They are involved with redefinitions of the universe of voters, political parties, and the broad boundaries of the politically possible.

To recapitulate, then, eras of critical realignment are marked by short, sharp reorganizations of the mass coalitional bases of the major parties which occur at periodic intervals on the national level; are often preceded by major third-party revolts which reveal the incapacity of "politics as usual" to integrate, much less aggregate, emergent political demand; are closely associated with abnormal stress in the socioeconomic system; are marked by ideological polarizations and issue-distances between the major parties which are exceptionally large by normal standards; and have durable consequences as constituent acts which determine the outer boundaries of policy in general, though not necessarily of policies in detail.

---

[15] The most obviously plausible example of synchronization of institutional-role and policy-output change with critical realignment is the Supreme Court of the United States. The literature is voluminous if frequently inferential, and the subject merits a more explicit relational treatment than it has received. For an excellent account of elite attitudes under the pressure of the crisis of the 1890's and the enormous impetus this gave to judicial creativity in this period, see Arnold M. Paul, *Conservative Crisis and the Rule of Law* (Ithaca, N.Y.: Cornell University Press, 1960).

2

The Periodicity of American Critical Realignments

When one speaks of party "systems" over time in the United States, it is of importance to note that the term relates primarily to what might be called voting systems or electoral-politics systems rather than to organizational structures. This is particularly so if the discussion is rooted in analysis of voting behavior, as it is here. For so far as American party organizations are concerned, it may legitimately be said that on one level they have undergone no basic transformations since they achieved characteristic form in the 1840's, but that on another level transformations in party structures have occurred with great frequency at certain periods of American political history. Even if one discriminates between "party systems" as essentially voting systems on the one hand and organizational systems on the other (and the tendency to confusion here is typically American), there is considerable uncertainty in the literature as to whether American electoral history can be legitimately or meaningfully partitioned into eras or periods in the first place, and what the nature and implications of such partitioning would be in the second.

The problem is perhaps not as acute for earlier periods of American electoral history: it is widely accepted that there was a first party system lasting from about 1793 to about 1816, an interregnum of no-party politics known as the "Era of Good Feeling," and a second party system which emerged after 1828 and was terminated by the Kansas-Nebraska Act of 1854 and the Civil War.[1] In organizational terms, there is something to be said for the view that the second system was followed by a third, with Democratic and Republican parties as major components, and that this system has remained largely unchanged ever since except for such Progressive-era modifications as the direct primary.

Identity of labels, however, is far from being the same as identity of contents: when Grover Cleveland said in 1900 that "the Democratic Party as we knew it is dead," he spoke from an existential perspective which latter-day analysis can verify. Similar sentiments were expressed by Jouett Shouse, Al Smith, and Newton D. Baker in the 1930's and 1940's, and with equally good empirical justification: they were leaders who had been shunted aside, if not discredited, in the aftermath of realignment.[2]

As we have noted above, a prime characteristic of realignment in the voting or electoral-politics system is a basic and measurable transformation in the shape of that voting universe.

[1] For useful discussions of interest to political scientists as well as historians, see Lee Benson, *The Concept of Jacksonian Democracy* (Princeton, N.J.: Princeton University Press, 1961), especially pp. 3–109; and Richard P. McCormick, *The Second American Party System* (Chapel Hill: University of North Carolina Press, 1966).

[2] A provocative discussion of this leadership displacement within the Democratic Party during the 1890's is found in J. Rogers Hollingsworth, *The Whirligig of Politics* (Chicago: University of Chicago Press, 1963), especially pp. 52–83, 156–71.

Such transformations may involve the development of clusters of local oppositions whose origins may often be obscured in the mists of local history, as was the case in the step-by-step emergence of the second party system in the 1828–40 period; or heavy regional polarizations, such as those emerging in the 1850's; or the struggles between America's Southern and Western economic "colonies" and the industrially dominant Northeastern "metropole," which assumed central political importance from the 1890's to the 1930's; or a mixture of class and ethnic polarizations with a broadly nationalizing focus, as in the 1928–36 realignment. But whatever the specific dominant focus of realignment may be, measurable universe change at a temporal cutting point or points ought to be present.

At least two complementary—though differently derived—measurement techniques can be employed longitudinally in such a way as to identify "cutting points" of transition between one system of electoral politics and another.

The first line of these, the "discontinuity variable," has been suggested by Mordecai Ezekiel and Karl A. Fox.[3] A regression line is mathematically fitted for the entire time period under consideration and residuals are derived for each election in the series. As modified for use here, ten presidential elections are taken in sequence, with the plotting of five 0's followed by five 1's on the X axis and appropriate residuals from a regression line, which is usually based on the percentage Democratic of the two-party vote.[4] In other words, ten elections are evaluated at a time, with clear transition between the first five and the last five. If a systematic change in residual values appears at any point, this will be reflected in a discontinuity coefficient (r_d),

[3] Mordecai Ezekiel and Karl A. Fox, *Methods of Correlation and Regression Analysis*, 3rd ed. (New York: Wiley & Sons, 1959), pp. 343–44.
[4] The exceptions to this rule fall in 1848, 1856, 1860, 1892, 1912, 1924, and 1968. In all cases except that of 1860, the Democratic percentage used here is of the three-party vote. In 1860 the northern and southern Democratic percentages of the total national vote are summed together.

which will tend to approximate unity; if random fluctuation or
no change occurs, the coefficient will tend to approximate
zero.[5] Having evaluated the coefficient for the first ten elections in the sequence, we then proceed to delete the earliest
residual, add the residual for the election next following the
last in the original sequence, move the cutting point forward
one election, and repeat the process until all possible sequences
of ten contiguous elections are evaluated. The implicit hypothesis is that critical-realignment years should be associated
with coefficients which are, when squared, both high and
"knife-edged," viewed longitudinally.

Similarly, one can employ the t test for differences between
means. This argument could be couched in probabilistic terms.
In any given sequence within an ongoing behavioral system,
fluctuations in residuals should be the result not of systemic
change but of random influences which, viewed longitudinally,
will tend to cancel out: either the two means being evaluated
will be nearly identical or the differences between them will
be largely accounted for by differences in their standard deviations. The converse hypothesis—that significant changes in
state occur within this system over time, and perhaps periodically—should be supported by the generation of t values too
high to be reasonably the product of chance or random fluctuations.

Since the size of these values is closely associated with the
assumptions underlying the original measurement, it is important to state the latter. The percentage Democratic of the
two-party vote is the base of the regression line, with two
exceptions: in 1856 and 1860, where the percentage of Democratic (combined northern and southern Democratic in 1860)
of the three-party vote was employed, since the Whig Party,
while superseded as the second major party by the realign-

[5] As Ezekiel and Fox point out, "A significant net regression coefficient
implies a significant change in the relationship from one period to the
other." (*Op. cit.*, p. 344.)

ment of 1854–60, was not entirely extinguished until the outbreak of the Civil War; and in 1912, where the Democratic percentage of the three-party vote corresponds most accurately to its share of the major-party vote as well. The results of these evaluations, under these assumptions, are presented in Table 2.1.

An examination of Table 2.1 reveals two things: a very close positive association between the values of t and r_d^2 and the fact that only very few of the twenty-seven arrays which cover the period from 1828 through 1968 show high values of either. If one accepts a one-tailed t test at the 0.025 level, the midpoint years which show values above those that might be attributed to chance are 1854, 1874, 1894, and 1930, with eight degrees of freedom. If one moves to the 0.01 level, 1854 barely fails to qualify, while all the others far exceed the 2.896 value of t at that cutting point. All the others, with the possible exception of the series with midpoint year 1926, fall far below the threshold of chance variation, and this one case can be accurately enough regarded as fitting within the complex pattern of realignment which was to culminate a few years later with the emergence of the New Deal.

With the exception of the extremely high 1874 figure, a striking periodicity is visible in the array taken as a whole: from 1854 to 1894 is a period of forty years, between 1894 and 1930 thirty-six years. Two anomalies, however, need some explanation: the relatively low values of r_d^2 and t for 1854, and the spectacularly high figures of both for 1874. Without attempting to explain away inconvenient data, it can be argued that both figures reveal certain peculiarities of realignment which were associated with the Civil War period.

In the first place, the reorganization of politics in the 1850's involved the collapse and eventual disappearance of one of the two major parties. If one evaluates by a t test the percentage Democratic of the two-party Democratic-Whig vote—which this unique event in our history would justify in some degree

Table 2.1 Evidence of Periodicity in Voting-System
Change: Discontinuity Variables Over Time on the
National Level, 1828–1968

$$(Y_c = 48.83 + 0.01\,X)$$

Period	Midpoint Year	r_d	r_d^2	t
1828–1864	1846	−.544	.296	1.836
1832–1868	1850	−.369	.137	1.125
1836–1872	1854	−.708	.501	2.832
1840–1876	1858	−.292	.085	0.864
1844–1880	1862	−.242	.059	0.705
1848–1884	1866	+.131	.017	0.374
1852–1888	1870	+.231	.053	0.670
1856–1892	1874	+.908	.824	6.120
1860–1896	1878	+.575	.331	1.988
1864–1900	1882	+.362	.131	1.097
1868–1904	1886	−.184	.034	0.529
1872–1908	1890	−.402	.161	1.241
1876–1912	1894	−.821	.674	4.065
1880–1916	1898	−.602	.363	2.134
1884–1920	1902	−.586	.344	2.047
1888–1924	1906	−.371	.137	1.256
1892–1928	1910	−.397	.157	1.223
1896–1932	1914	−.028	.001	0.078
1900–1936	1918	+.059	.003	0.167
1904–1940	1922	+.385	.149	1.181
1908–1944	1926	+.666	.443	2.522
1912–1948	1930	+.817	.668	4.015
1916–1952	1934	+.496	.246	1.614
1920–1956	1938	+.143	.020	0.408
1924–1960	1942	−.133	.018	0.381
1928–1964	1946	−.311	.097	0.925
1932–1968	1950	−.546	.298	1.844

—the result, of course, would be a peak value slightly in excess of 7 at midpoint 1858, followed by a decline to 0 by midpoint 1882.

Secondly, while the Democratic Party lost key elements of its support during the realignment of the 1850's—with its share of the presidential vote remaining somewhat artificially depressed through 1872—its coalitional base outside the South and outside areas of rural New England settlement remained very largely intact through and after the Civil War. In this respect, the great upsurge of r_d and t associated with midpoint year 1874 reflects both the re-emergence of Democratic ascendancy in the South and the party's nonsouthern upsurge associated with the depression of 1873–79.

Thus, what followed after the realignment of 1874–76 was what might justifiably be called the third, or Civil War, party system in its "normal" or stable phase; if in this instance the achievement of "normal" conditions took the form of two realignments approximately twenty years apart, it reflects the unparalleled magnitude of the shock then administered to the system of American electoral politics. In short, these "seismic" peculiarities of the period reflect an underlying reality of American politics in that period of which leaders of Radical Reconstruction were only too aware, and in response to which their political strategy emerged: the durability of the party which opposed the Republican revolution by force of arms in the South and more covertly though with scarcely less determination in the North.

The profile of long-term stability and short-term disruption which emerged from this treatment of electoral behavior at the global national level is particularly striking when the tendency of sharp regionally based polarizations to cancel themselves out at this level is considered. So far as the national behavioral system is concerned, it is evident that sharp readjustments of partisan boundaries have recurred at remark-

in turnout, which in our series analysis begins at midpoint year 1890, reaches a very high plateau—rather than a peak—at midpoint 1898. This plateau continues until midpoint 1910, which indicates a continuing and very massive process of turnout decline associated with the "system of 1896," about which we shall have more to say subsequently.

Similarly, reversal of this downward trend, visible at midpoint year 1922, reaches its crest in midpoint years 1930 and 1934—that is, at the point of transition from the fourth to the fifth party systems. As can be seen from the regression lines at the bottom of Table 2.3, this most recent transformation in turnout rates has an upward slope which is far smaller than the downward slope of the 1896–1928 period. But the high and positive regression coefficient for the period with midpoint year 1950 indicates that the process of remobilization of the mass electorate, which had as many downs as ups during the 1928–48 period, has been stabilized at a moderately high level—that is, at about the level of 1912 and 1916—since the first Eisenhower election.[9] Thus, in general it can be said that the use of this analytical technique over an extended time series yields temporally compatible results as between party voting and gross political participation, but quite different specific patterns. The first reveals considerable evidence of semidiscontinuous jumps in universe state; the second points to a much more extended process of systemic change, but a process which clearly has a significant relationship of some kind to the partisan data.

Let us turn to a similar analysis of change in partisan-vote patterns at the state level. Selected sets of contiguous elections and midpoints for six northern states have been ex-

---

[9] It is also worth noting in passing that this highly positive turnout coefficient for the period with midpoint year 1950 is associated with an increase in the negative Democratic-percentage-based coefficient for the same period found in Table 2.1.

Table 2.3 Transformations at the National Level: Turnout, 1824–1968

Period	Midpoint Year	Mean Turnout		t
		M_1	M_2	
1824–1860	1842	55.6	76.3	2.362
1828–1864	1846	66.0	75.2	2.112
1832–1868	1850	69.0	76.3	1.301
1836–1872	1854	71.8	76.7	1.095
1840–1876	1858	76.1	77.2	0.404
1844–1880	1862	76.3	76.9	0.214
1848–1884	1866	75.2	77.6	0.869
1852–1888	1870	76.3	77.9	0.567
1856–1892	1874	76.7	78.5	0.875
1860–1896	1878	77.2	78.0	0.356
1864–1900	1882	76.9	76.8	0.035
1868–1904	1886	77.6	74.3	1.050
1872–1908	1890	77.9	71.6	1.926
1876–1912	1894	78.5	68.4	2.710
1880–1916	1898	78.0	64.8	5.104
1884–1920	1902	76.8	60.0	5.207
1888–1924	1906	74.3	56.8	4.166
1892–1928	1910	71.6	55.1	4.379
1896–1932	1914	68.4	54.7	3.162
1900–1936	1918	64.8	54.6	3.022
1904–1940	1922	60.0	57.2	0.737
1908–1944	1926	56.8	58.6	0.521
1912–1948	1930	55.1	57.9	0.897
1916–1952	1934	54.7	59.1	1.399
1920–1956	1938	54.6	59.1	1.446
1924–1960	1942	57.2	59.4	0.666
1928–1964	1946	58.6	60.5	0.803
1932–1968	1950	57.9	62.1	2.255

Table 2.4 Comparisons of Discriminant Scores Among
Six States: Selected Midpoint Years, 1891–1957 *

Ten Continguous Elections	Mid-point	Indiana		Massachusetts		Michigan	
		r_d	r_d^2	r_d	r_d^2	r_d	r_d^2
1882/1900	1891	−.689	.475	−.696	.484	−.790	.625
1884/1902	1893	−.850	.723	−.921	.849	−.910	.827
1886/1904	1895	−.538	.290	−.874	.763	−.582	.339
1888/1906	1897	−.526	.277	−.473	.224	−.646	.417
1894/1912	1903	+.086	.007	+.389	.151	−.781	.610
1900/1918	1909	+.146	.021	+.433	.187	+.016	.000
1902/1920	1911	−.305	.093	−.124	.015	−.199	.040
1904/1922	1913	−.209	.044	−.206	.042	+.090	.008
1908/1926	1917	−.419	.175	+.475	.226	−.658	.433
1910/1928	1919	−.288	.083	−.472	.223	−.782	.612
1918/1936	1927	+.618	.382	+.867	.752	+.557	.310
1920/1938	1929	+.815	.664	+.671	.451	+.791	.625
1922/1940	1931	+.623	.388	+.438	.192	+.930	.865
1932/1950	1941	−.716	.513	−.202	.041	−.650	.422
1934/1952	1943	−.508	.258	−.028	.001	−.503	.253
1944/1962	1953	+.368	.136	+.266	.071	+.646	.417
1946/1964	1955	+.445	.198	+.419	.176	+.570	.324
1948/1966	1957	+.531	.282	+.308	.095	+.374	.140

amined for the period 1880–1966/68. The rules have been
modified somewhat from the national data analysis just presented. The percentage Democratic of the vote [10] is the mean
for all statewide political offices in each election.[11] The time
interval is contracted to a two-year span, including off-year

[10] This is the Democratic percentage of the two-party vote except for
Wisconsin, where, because of the 1934–42 third-party (Progressive)
phenomenon, the Democratic percentage of the total vote has been used.
In all the other states, the Democratic percentage of the three-party vote
has also been used for 1912–14.

[11] See Tables 1–5 in the Appendix.

Ten Contiguous Elections	Mid-point	Pennsylvania		Rhode Island		Wisconsin	
		r_d	r_d^2	r_d	r_d^2	r_d	r_d^2
1882/1900	1891	−.785	.616	−.367	.135	−.581	.337
1884/1902	1893	−.917	.841	−.692	.479	−.832	.692
1886/1904	1895	−.662	.439	−.825	.680	−.690	.476
1888/1906	1897	−.565	.320	−.599	.358	−.664	.441
1894/1912	1903	−.685	.469	+.147	.022	−.396	.157
1900/1918	1909	−.040	.002	−.597	.357	+.028	.001
1902/1920	1911	+.291	.085	−.651	.424	−.206	.043
1904/1922	1913	+.398	.159	−.350	.122	−.523	.273
1908/1926	1917	−.434	.189	−.260	.068	−.868	.754
1910/1928	1919	−.384	.148	−.180	.032	−.786	.618
1918/1936	1927	+.646	.418	+.650	.423	+.695	.482
1920/1938	1929	+.737	.543	+.517	.268	+.491	.241
1922/1940	1931	+.903	.815	+.484	.234	+.448	.201
1932/1950	1941	−.458	.210	+.366	.134	+.183	.033
1934/1952	1943	−.412	.170	+.128	.016	+.783	.613
1944/1962	1953	+.454	.206	−.381	.145	+.705	.497
1946/1964	1955	+.408	.166	−.277	.075	+.669	.448
1948/1966	1957	+.402	.161	−.316	.099	+.761	.580

* Based on mean percentage Democratic of the two-party vote for all offices in each election year, except in Wisconsin, where, because of special three-party conditions in the 1934–44 period, the percentage Democratic of the total vote was used.

elections. Correspondingly, it is half as long as the national. Of course, this should serve to increase "background noise" from off-year state election results somewhat, but it also should provide quite similar quantitative indices of realignment to those developed for the national level. The data are presented in Table 2.4, omitting election sequences with low coefficients.

A table such as this suggests at once how complex electoral movement over time becomes when we move to the state level —a complexity which becomes even more humbling when smaller geographical areas of analysis are employed. Even so, there are several patterns which stand out with some clarity from the array. In the first place, there are two—and only two —periods in which the coefficients generally approach unity: those with 1893/95 and 1927/31 as cutting points. Even here there is obviously considerable variation. For example, Rhode Island shows a midpoint peak somewhat later in the 1890's than do the other states.

More impressively, and very suggestive of the more complex, diffuse character of the New Deal realignment, the peaks for this period are both relatively more uneven as between the states and fall at several midpoints in the series: Massachusetts, Rhode Island, and Wisconsin in 1927, Indiana in 1929, and Pennsylvania and Michigan in 1931. The early appearance of realignment peaks in the two New England states seems clearly to flow from the merger of the "Al Smith Revolution" of 1928 with the pro-Democratic reinforcement provided by the 1929 Depression and the New Deal itself. Wisconsin is essentially in a class by itself, since what might have begun as a realignment of state politics along national lines in 1932 was aborted for more than a decade by the rise of the La Follette family party, the Wisconsin Progressives. This is faithfully reflected in the appearance of *1943* as the realignment cutting point in that state.

It seems evident from the arrays in other periods that no comparable uniformity of movement exists; moreover, squared coefficients of comparable magnitude tend to be scattered and are evidently associated with local rather than national political effects. This is particularly true of the period around 1912, which has sometimes been thought of as a realigning period.[12] Not only is there no midpoint year in this period (1909–13) in which all coefficient signs are either positive or negative, but— with the exception of Rhode Island, where local movements were both deviant and pro-Republican [13]—the squared co-efficients are uniformly very small even with a narrowly spaced two-year span between contiguous election sets.[14] One can find similar cross-cutting at work in the period with midpoints 1941–43—relatively heavily anti-Democratic in Indiana, Michigan, and Pennsylvania, little evidence of discontinuity in Massachusetts, and faintly pro-Democratic in Rhode Island and Wisconsin.

The closest post-1931 successor to the great realignment peaks described above is found in the period with cutting points from 1953 through 1957, with all states but Rhode Island showing some evidence of pro-Democratic shift. In two cases the squared coefficients in this period are fairly substantial: Michigan (1953) and Wisconsin (1953 and 1957), and this corresponds to the pronounced pro-Democratic movement in the northern tier of states during the mid-1950's which has been mentioned in the literature.[15] Even here, however,

[12] See, for instance, Charles G. Sellers, "The Equilibrium Cycle in Two-Party Politics," 30 *Public Opinion Quarterly*, pp. 16–38 (1965).

[13] This seems, among other things, to be associated with the Republican wooing of the French-Canadian vote and the gubernatorial candidacy of Aram J. Pothier. See Duane Lockard, *New England State Politics* (Princeton, N.J.: Princeton University Press, 1959), pp. 172–77.

[14] The justification for employing the Democratic percentage of the three-party vote in 1912 and 1914 rests essentially upon behavioral rather than upon election outcome or policy grounds. The Progressive vote, so far as one can ascertain at this preliminary stage of analysis, was derived overwhelmingly—probably about 95 per cent or more—from voters normally part of the Republican coalition prior to 1910 and after 1916. Since it is realignment as a *behavioral* phenomenon which is studied here, it was considered appropriate to treat the great Republican Party split of 1912 and its aftermath accordingly.

[15] See, for example, Duane Lockard's discussion of Maine in Lockard, *op. cit.*, pp. 101–7; and Richard E. Dawson, "Social Development, Party

the coefficients lag far behind their levels in the two national realignments, and elsewhere they tend to be quite small.[16]

Finally, while the period with midpoint year 1919 reveals uniformity in coefficient signs, the extreme spread in the squares of the coefficients (from .032 in Rhode Island to .618 in Wisconsin) provides some evidence for the view that the 1918–20 shift toward the Republicans and "normalcy," great as it was, did not really lead to any uniform changes in state of the sort one associates with the concept "realignment."

Gerald Pomper has argued that realignment sequences are not truly cyclical—that is, they do not recur after a precise number of years has passed.[17] He is surely correct in this argument, as in his assertion that major third-party campaigns are often associated with realignments. Nevertheless, there is much evidence—some of it presented in Tables 2.2 and 2.3— that realignments do recur with rather remarkable regularity approximately once a generation, or every thirty to thirty-eight years.

The precise timing of the conditions which conduce to realignment is conditioned heavily by circumstance, of course: the intrusion of major crises in society and economy with

Competition, and Policy," in Chambers and Burnham, *op. cit.*, pp. 203–37, and especially at p. 226.

[16] Two further cases may be noted. In Michigan and Pennsylvania— which tend in many ways to show marked aggregate similarities throughout the 1880–1968 period—the realignment which was set in motion in the mid-1890's was further accelerated around 1904. In both states the swing toward Theodore Roosevelt in the 1904 landslide was abnormally large and had considerable aftereffects for the structure of party competition. In this respect they appear to resemble California's post-1896 pattern. See Rogin, *op. cit.* Both of these two states reveal moderately high r_d for the ten-election period with 1903 as midpoint; and both were carried (as was California) by Roosevelt in 1912. In Wisconsin, on the other hand, there was an extremely strong temporal discrepancy, again with pro-Republican direction, in the ten-election sequence with 1917 as midpoint year. It seems fair to say that the net effect of the Wilson Administration's involvement in World War I was to complete the ruin of the Democratic Party in this heavily German state. But this effect, while obviously intense and durable, was vastly more intense locally than nationally.

[17] Pomper, *op. cit.*, pp. 560–61.

which "politics as usual" in the United States cannot adequately cope, and the precise quality and bias of leadership decisions in a period of high political tension, cannot be predicted in specific time with any accuracy. Yet a broadly repetitive pattern of oscillation between the normal inertia of mass electoral politics and the ruptures of the normal which realignments bring about is clearly evident from the data. So evident is this pattern that one is led to suspect that the truly "normal" structure of American electoral politics at the mass base is precisely this dynamic, even dialectic polarization between long-term inertia and concentrated bursts of change in this open system of action. It may well be that American political institutions, including the major political parties, are so organized that they have a chronic, cumulative tendency toward underproduction of other than currently "normal" policy outputs. They may tend persistently to ignore, and hence not to aggregate, emergent political demand of a mass character until a boiling point of some kind is reached.

In this context, the rise of third-party protests as what might be called protorealignment phenomena would be associated with the repeated emergence of a rising gap between perceived expectations of the political process and its perceived realities over time, diffused among a constantly increasing portion of the active electorate and perhaps mobilizing many hitherto inactive voters. Such parties have been associated with the initial stages of every realignment from the 1830's to—perhaps—1968.

But here, rather clearly, distinctions must be made as between two basic types of large-scale third-party activity. One type is the major-party bolt, which, organizationally and at the mass base, detaches the most acutely disaffected parts of a major party's coalition. As a rule, such parties are only with difficulty associated with a subsequent realignment which *durably* changes the coalitional structures of the major parties. The other variety may be described more accurately as a protest movement which may for a time have broad appeal, which is usually staffed by cadres not prominent in either major-party establishment, and which draws mass support cutting across pre-existing party lines.

It can be tentatively suggested that when such parties reach 5 per cent or more of the total national vote they are more likely than not either to be proximately associated with realignment or to fall in periods of relatively high tension which are located about midway in the life cycle of an electoral era. Classification at this stage must remain largely impressionistic until the correlates of significant third-party voting are examined in detail. But it would be reasonable to suggest the following as significant third parties of the latter type: Anti-Masonic, 1832; Free Soil, 1848; Greenback, 1878; Populist, 1892–94; Socialist, 1912; La Follette Progressive, 1924; American Independent (Wallace), 1968.[18]

At least two characteristic patterns emerge from this array. In the first place, there seems a fairly clear and again recurrent relationship between these parties and subsequent realignments: between the Anti-Masonic Party in the northeastern states and the emergence of the second party system

[18] Of the borderline cases, the most obvious are the American (1856) and the Constitutional Union (1860), which clearly had a non-Democratic, non-Republican mass base. Here, however, the classification must be evident. These—along with all of the "opposition" parties of various shades in the slave states from 1855 to 1860—were the fragments of the deceased Whig Party, not finally extinguished as separate entities until the Civil War. The La Follette movement was clearly enough a "bridge" to critical realignment, even in nonfarm states. (See text, pp. 55–57.) The Wallace movement of 1968, since it drew such a large share of its national vote from normally Democratic electoral strongholds, is also in some respects a borderline case. But in states such as Pennsylvania it fulfills the suggested requirements: 8 per cent of the total vote; leadership not drawn from high-visibility positions in either of the major parties; and virtually zero correlation with both 1960 and 1964 county percentages and the most obvious demographic attributes. See Walter Dean Burnham and John D. Sprague, "Additive and Multiplicative Models of the Voting Universe: The Case of Pennsylvania, 1960–1968," in the June 1970 issue of the *American Political Science Review*.

there; [19] between the Free Soil Party and the collapse of that system; [20] between the Populist upsurge and the realignments of the mid-1890's; and between the La Follette Progressives and the reorganization of American electoral politics which began to emerge in 1928. The Greenback and Socialist peaks fell almost midpoint in the electoral eras in which they occurred. The latter case coincided, of course, with the Bull Moose split in the Republican Party. Also, a generally "party-bolt" pair of splits from the Democratic Party in 1948 seems to have occurred about midway between the beginning of the fifth major electoral era and what may well be its end-point in the late 1960's. Such midpoint indicators of tension, no less than the protorealignment third-party protests themselves, are further indicators of the interplay in American politics between the *vis inertiae* of "normal" political routines once established and pressure arising from the rapidity, unevenness, and uncontrolled character of change in the country's dynamic socioeconomic system.

Secondly, all the protorealignment parties except for the Wallace movement of 1968 had a "leftist" orientation for their time. They constituted attacks by groups who felt they were outsiders against an elite whom they frequently viewed in conspiratorial terms. These attacks were made in the name of democratic-humanistic universals against an established political structure which was perceived to be corrupt, undemocratic, and manipulated by insiders for their and their sup-

[19] See Benson, *op. cit.*, pp. 21–46.

[20] See McCormick's comments on the short-lived character of the second party system in its mature phase. (McCormick, *op. cit.*, pp. 353–56.) There is much behavioral data, in both the deep southern and far northern states during the 1847–51 period, to support the view that leadership decisions which fashioned the Compromise of 1850 barely averted its collapse at that time, and still more interesting data from Ohio and Connecticut in 1853 which suggests an impending collapse of the Whig Party and a corresponding rise in Free Soil strength even before the introduction of the Kansas-Nebraska Act in Congress.

porters' benefit.[21] All of them were perceived by their followers as "movements" which would not only purify the corruption of the present political regime but replace some of its
most important constituent parts. Moreover, they all "tele-
graphed," as it were, the basic issue-clusters which would
dominate politics in the next electoral era: the completion of
political democratization in the 1830's, slavery and sectionalism
in the late 1840's and 1850's, the struggle between metropole
and colonial regions in the 1890's, welfare liberalism vs.
laissez-faire in the 1920's and 1930's.

The argument may be broadened somewhat by noting that
significant third parties of the cross-cutting "movement" type
have all entailed expressions of acute center-periphery tension
at the polls. The nineteenth-century parties, without exception, were solidly rural in their mass base, if not in their leadership; they tended to be evangelical in religion and radically
democratic in their political demands. As such, they correspond
rather closely in demands and clienteles, if not in longevity, to
fundamentalist-agrarian movements in European—and particularly Scandinavian—multiparty systems. The major protest parties of this century, while not so unambiguously rural,
remain heavily periphery-oriented. This was true to a degree
even of the Socialists of 1912, for while Eugene Debs' following was heavy among the garment-trade immigrants of
New York's Lower East Side and the Germans of Milwaukee,
his largest countywide totals were registered in such colonial
areas as the mountain states, Oklahoma, and Huey Long's
Louisiana birthplace, Winn Parish.[22]

All this suggests a relationship of significance between the
periodic recurrence of third-party forerunners of realignment
—and realignments themselves—and certain dominant pecu-

[21] Precisely, of course, as was the case with the insurgent movement
of 1968 which did *not* crystallize as a third party, the McCarthy movement against the Democratic "establishment." See Wildavsky, *op. cit.*
[22] There seems something almost quintessentially periphery-protest ori-

liarities of polity and society in the United States. It can be argued that center-periphery conflict has been a major part of every realignment in the United States, and was probably dominant in all but the last. This may only be another way of restating the conventional hypotheses as to the diversity of American politics and the heterogeneity of political coalitions in this country. But what is most striking about this pattern, so markedly re-enacted in the 1964 and 1968 elections, is that it periodically recurs.

Such horizontal segmentation corresponds to a political system in which a sense of common nationhood may be much more nearly skin-deep than is usually appreciated. If there is any evolutionary scale of political modernization at all, the pervasive dominance of horizontal fault lines in electoral politics, in which antagonisms of political subcultures and those arising from American variants of the "colonial situation" play so large a role, suggest quite strongly that the United States is still a "new nation" in some important political respects. The periodic recurrence of these tensions as system-dominant may also imply that—as dynamically developed as our economic system is—no convincing evidence of *political* development in the United States can be found for any period after the

---

ented about the political behavior of Winn Parish. To illustrate from selected presidential elections:

Year	% Democratic	% Republican	% Other
1880	100.0	–	–
1892	21.4	–	78.6 (Populist-Republican fusion)
1912	56.8	7.1	35.1 (Socialist)
1932	98.4	1.6	–
1948	32.2	11.4	56.4 (States' Rights)
1952	53.5	46.5	–
1956	35.0	49.6	15.4 (States' Rights)
1960	27.1	44.9	28.0 (States' Rights)
1964	21.5	78.5	–
1968	19.5	16.7	63.8 (Wallace)

1830's, or at the latest the 1860's.

Finally it should be emphasized that in analyzing the basic element of periodicity in American electoral behavior, realignments should be regarded as involving rapid, compressed jumps in universe state, *irrespective of the partisan direction of those jumps.* One recent contribution to the literature of classification of presidential elections argues for a division of elections with durable aftereffects into "converting" and "realigning." Thus it is argued that the 1896 realignment was "converting," since it reinforced a Republican majority status which had been in existence since 1860.[23]

One may object to this classification scheme on two grounds. In the first place, the 1874–92 period was precisely one in which—uniquely in a hundred and forty years of electoral history—there was in fact no national majority for either party. That period corresponds pretty closely to the Civil War, or third, electoral era in its "normal" state, with the temporary distortions imposed by the immediate wartime period removed. While it is of course true that Republicans controlled the presidency throughout much the largest part of the 1860–92 period, this has more relevance to elite and policy analysis than to coalitional or behavioral analysis. For while the Republicans after 1864 did win the presidency on all but two occasions, it was also characteristically true that between 1874 and 1892 the Democrats won pluralities of the national vote nine times compared with one for the Republicans, and won control of the House of Representatives eight times compared with two for the Republicans.

In the second place, and of equal importance, the direction of realignment is less significant in the analysis of behavior than its occurrence and duration. Critical elections may have the net effect of coverting a hitherto one-party state into a competitive battleground, as happened in Missouri during and

[23] Pomper, *op. cit.*, p. 538 *et seq.*

after the realignment of the 1890's, or of converting a state with a normal but narrow party majority into one whose voters realign overwhelmingly toward that party. To argue that nationally or locally the first should be described as "realigning" and the second as "converting," for example, seems merely to advocate the addition of superfluous typologies and thus to make analysis perhaps more complex than is necessary.

3

The Nature of Electoral Change: The Case of Pennsylvania

With the foregoing discussion in mind, let us now turn to a closer, long-range examination of voting behavior in one major American state, Pennsylvania. While the primary focus of analysis will be the period from 1875 to 1968, some attention will be paid to earlier patterns of alignment at the global state level. No claim can be made that Pennsylvania is somehow typical of the country as a whole, but its political evolution over the past century takes on added interest precisely because of its great size, its early and massive industrialization, and its present very high level of socioeconomic development.

The earlier electoral history of this state seems to have been rather inchoate; not until just before the election of 1840 did its electoral and party alignments come to parallel those of the second party system generally. Indeed, it can be said that this

34

national system did not become fully matured until states like Pennsylvania had become integrated into it. Its basic mid-nineteenth-century partisan alignments were laid down in a period when Pennsylvania was still overwhelmingly agrarian: 82.1 per cent of its population was still rural at the time of the 1840 census. Once brought into being—here as elsewhere a heterogeneous mass of local antagonisms, many of whose origins remain obscure to this day—this alignment system entailed a very full mobilization of the adult white male population. Moreover, it was closely competitive at the state level, and it endured for many decades with slight change at the mass base.

As it well known, during the post-Jacksonian phase of the second party system Pennsylvania was intensely competitive, but with a Democratic predominance which, if narrow, was usually decisive: of sixteen statewide and presidential contests between 1836 and 1854, Democrats won eleven. The subsequent realignment of the 1850's was remarkable for two things: it was extremely limited in scope, and it was sufficient to give the new Republican Party a narrow edge which was both normally decisive and of vital importance to the party's objectives. As the summary discussion of periodicity at the end of this chapter makes evident, one result of this was an extremely limited upswing in the values of t during the 1850's.

We cannot attempt an exhaustive review here of all of the possible factors which may have contributed to the conversion of Pennsylvania from a normally and narrowly Democratic state during the second party system to a normally but narrowly Republican one during the third, but several aspects of the problem can be explored. The overriding reality appears to have been that by the time the oscillations associated with realignment ceased around 1862, the Republicans had inherited the Whig mass base almost intact while the Democrats had managed, on the whole, to preserve theirs through the storm.

The Democratic percentages of the two-party vote by county for the 1852 and 1864 elections, for example, correlate at +.678.[1] Since sharp breaks toward the Republicans were heavily concentrated in counties of New England-New York population concentrations, this figure considerably understates the degree of durability which existed in the rest of the state's electorate during this period. If one extracts the ten counties whose 1870 native populations included 10 per cent or more born in New York, for example, the 1852–64 Democratic correlation for the remaining fifty-three counties reaches +.886.[2]

Viewed in global terms, the decisive margins of Republican victory after 1856 were provided by the New England-origin counties—the only area in the state where pro-Republican coversion of former Democrats appears to have occurred on a mass scale—and by the two major urban centers. Indeed, the capstone seems to have been placed on the Republican margin by the party's capture of Philadelphia, a fact which had much to do with the development of that city's celebrated machine politics. Some measure of the contributions to realignment in Pennsylvania during the 1850's can be provided by examining, in Table 3.1, the 1840–64 results in the two urban counties, the ten counties with large concentrations of New York natives, six counties with large Pennsylvania German populations,[3] and the remainder of the state.

[1] Variance explained: 46.01 per cent.

[2] Variance explained: 78.48 per cent. The ten counties in which persons of New York origin constituted 10 per cent or more of the native-stock population in 1870 are: Bradford, Crawford, Erie, McKean, Potter, Susquehanna, Tioga, Venango, Warren, and Wayne. It is worth noting that the correlation of percentages Democratic in 1852 and 1864 yields an r of only +.246 for these ten counties, which explains a mere 6.04 per cent of the variance.

[3] The "German" counties selected here are: Berks, Lancaster, Lebanon, Lehigh, Northampton, and York. While ordinary varieties of census data are not too helpful in isolating this ethnic element—its members' ancestors emigrated to Pennsylvania in Colonial times—one measure which may be used is the proportion of members of certain evangelical churches

Table 3.1 The Shift from the Second to the Third Party System: The Case of Pennsylvania, 1840–1864, and 1892

Percentage Democratic of the Total Vote

Year	Allegheny	Phila-delphia	10 New York Counties	6 German Counties	Rest of State	Whole State
1840	37.5	50.3	52.7	50.3	50.2	49.9
1844	40.3	44.5	55.1	51.5	51.7	50.5
1848	37.7	40.1	43.5	49.6	49.0	46.7
1852	40.6	50.8	51.8	51.0	52.5	51.2
1856	37.4	54.4	35.2	56.7	51.6	50.1
1860	29.5	40.0	32.1	45.4	43.4	41.1
1864	36.6	44.1	39.4	54.6	51.4	48.4
1892	39.4	41.7	38.1	51.5	47.2	45.5

Percentage of State Vote Cast in Each Area

1840	4.2	12.5	9.9	17.5	55.8	100.0
1864	5.9	17.4	11.5	14.7	50.6	100.0
1892	7.8	20.4	9.5	12.7	49.5	100.0

The pattern in Table 3.1 probably corresponds closely with those of a broad belt of middle states extending from New Jersey through Illinois, precisely the states where Lincoln's victory was forged in 1860, and in all cases by margins far narrower than Pennsylvania's.[4] In Pennsylvania, at any rate, the

of the church-going population. In the six counties mentioned here, 52 per cent of all church members in 1963 belonged to the Church of the Brethren, Evangelical United Brethren, the Lutheran Church, the United Church of Christ, and minor denominations of predominantly German origin such as the Mennonites. In the rest of Pennsylvania, only 14.2 per cent of the population attending church were members of these denominations. See *Pennsylvania Statistical Abstract 1964–65* (Harrisburg, 1965), pp. 10 and 19.

[4] Indeed, Lincoln's 1860 victory in Pennsylvania was itself deceptively large, and was largely the result of the breakdown of complex coalitional negotiations among his opponents. Thus, while he received 56.3 per cent of the total vote in November, the Republican candidate for governor at the October election won only 53.3 per cent in a two-man contest with a substantially fuller turnout.

Republican dominance of the third era was created out of marginal increments indeed: a hold in the urban counties comparable to that of the Whigs but with a constantly expanding relative size of the city electorate; and conversion in New England-settlement areas which was more than enough to compensate for some pro-Democratic movement in conservative German parts of the state. Elsewhere, for the most part, the alignment pattern shows astonishing invariance across this period. Indeed, it remains largely unchanged until the onset of the Depression of 1893. While a gradual pro-Republican secular trend is visible in the 1875–92 period, most of the increased Republican increment can be traced to the growing size of the party's pluralities in the two metropolitan counties as they underwent great expansion relative to the rest of the state. Much of the rest, it may be assumed, is associated with the dissemination of industrialization throughout Pennsylvania, particularly in the coal-mining areas.

The realignment of the 1893–96 period brought a decisive, abrupt end to this remarkably durable voting system and broke the state Democratic Party in the process. This sequence of transformation constituted a critical realignment in every behavioral sense of the term. One may begin by noting the great speed with which the break came: in the sequence of five annual elections from 1888 through November 1892, the mean percentage Democratic of the two-party vote was 46.7,[5] while for the five elections beginning in February 1894 the percentage was 37.8.[6] Clearly the triggering mechanism here was the onset of the second worst depression in the nation's

[5] The standard deviation of 1.46 was typically small for the period, and accurately reflects the extreme stability of electoral alignments in the last half of the third party system.

[6] The standard deviation here was even smaller: 0.79. If one applies a t test for difference of means for the two sets of elections before and after 1893, a score of 10.77 is derived. Such a score is at least five to ten times as large as it normally is in nonrealigning sequences.

history in 1893, with the Bryanite-colonial realignment *within* the Democratic Party serving to solidify this emergent distribution of electoral strength in this metropole state in and after 1896.

As in Key's New England towns, the impact of this realignment in Pennsylvania was heavily sectional. Thus most of the state's sixty-seven counties were moved with fairly uniform velocity in the same Republican direction. As a consequence, a very high continuity in the *relative* positioning of these counties was manifested, as Table 3.2 shows.

Table 3.2 Intercorrelations of County Percentages Democratic of the Two-Party Vote for all Pennsylvania Counties, 1892, 1896, and 1900

	1892	*1896*	*1900*
1892	1.000	+.921	+.946
1896	+.921	1.000	+.958
1900	+.946	+.958	1.000

A closer examination, however, reveals considerable internal differentiation in political responses within Pennsylvania to the great crisis of the 1890's. In the first instance, there is clearly a metropolitan-nonmetropolitan division, which is expressed in terms of maximum quantitative pro-Republican shift in the two major metropolitan areas, Allegheny and Philadelphia counties. Otherwise, however, these movements are not unambiguously related to at least the more obvious of quantifiable ecological characteristics. Thus a division of the state's counties along lines of urbanization [7] reveals the array for presidential elections in the 1884–1908 period shown in Table 3.3.

[7] The 1900 census definition of "urban" is employed here: that part of the population living in incorporated places of 2,500 or more inhabitants.

Table 3.3 Realignment in Pennsylvania: Percentage
Democratic of the Two-Party Vote by Levels of
Urbanization, 1884–1908

Year	11 Rural Counties (0% Urban 1900)		45 "Other" Counties (1–49.9% Urban)	
	% Dem. of 2-Party Vote	Net Dem. Shift	% Dem. of 2-Party Vote	Net Dem. Shift
1884	51.5		47.0	
1888	49.8	−1.7	46.4	−0.6
1892	50.2	+0.4	48.1	+1.7
1896	45.8	−4.4	41.4	−6.7
1900	45.5	−0.3	42.1	+0.7
1904	38.9	−6.6	33.9	−8.2
1908	43.3	+4.4	39.2	+5.7

Year	9 Urban Counties (50–82.8% Urban)		2 Metropolitan Counties (80–100% Urban)	
	% Dem. of 2-Party Vote	Net Dem. Shift	% Dem. of 2-Party Vote	Net Dem. Shift
1884	47.9		39.5	
1888	48.8	+0.9	42.9	+3.4
1892	50.5	+1.7	41.6	−1.3
1896	42.1	−8.4	26.7	−13.9
1900	44.0	+1.9	25.8	−0.9
1904	32.7	−11.3	18.1	−7.7
1908	45.5	+12.8	30.0	+11.9

Several points of interest emerge from this partitioning of
the state. The heavy contribution of the metropolitan areas to
Pennsylvania's statewide Republican majorities before 1894 is
clearly apparent, as is the general tendency for rural areas to
be associated with the Democratic Party of the third, or Civil
War, electoral-politics system. Similarly, the solidly rural
counties reveal far less net electoral change in and after 1896
than do counties in any more urbanized category. Indeed,
there is a visibly monotonic relationship between both the

degree of Democratic defection in 1896 and the mean partisan swing of the 1892/96–1904/08 period on one hand and the degree of urbanization on the other.[8] This, of course, reflects both the exceptional force of the realigning situation in the more industrialized parts of the state and the relative insulation of the more remote rural areas from the massive political tides which swept the state from 1894 through 1908. Even so, the monotonicity may be more apparent than real. For correlation of county percentages Democratic in 1892 and 1896 with their percentage of rural (or nonurbanized) population in 1900 yields an r of only +.184 for 1896. This is some improvement over the r of +.025 for the 1892 election, but neither coefficient shows much if any significance: even in 1896, gross rurality explains only 3 per cent of the variance in the Democratic vote.

One further aspect of realignment's aftermath is suggested in Table 3.3. While the percentage Democratic shows some tendency to increase after the 1896 trough in both the nine urban and two metropolitan counties, it reveals a continuing secular decline in the others. This decline is proportionately greatest precisely in the rural counties which had tended to support the Democratic Party during the Civil War alignment era. This movement tends to be confirmed for the whole subsequent period down through 1924: a correlation by county of the mean percentage Democratic for the 1876–92 period with the regression coefficient for 1908–24 yields an r of −.416.

[8] Application of the Democratic defection ratio for 1896 (in this case, $DDR = \dfrac{\text{Democratic Shift, 1892–96}}{\% \text{ Democratic, 1892}} \times 100$) and the mean partisan swing for the post-1892 period yields the following array:

Type of County	Number	Democratic Defection Ratio 1892–96	Mean Partisan Swing, 1892/96–1904/08
Rural	11	8.8	3.9
Intermediate	45	12.9	5.3
Urban	9	16.6	8.6
Metropolitan	2	33.4	8.6

Thus, a part of the complex process of critical realignment was the unleashing of a secular pro-Republican realignment thereafter among those "island community" counties which had been bastions of the nineteenth-century Democratic Party in Pennsylvania. The end-product of both critical and subsequent secular realignment, influenced as it was by such changes in the rules as the adoption of the direct primary in 1908, was the conversion of Pennsylvania into the stable Republican monolith of the 1920's.

Of additional interest in identifying the focus of realignment in this state during and after the 1890's is the identification of extreme cases on *political* rather than demographic grounds. A useful way to do this is to construct a regression line for each county's percentage Democratic in the 1876–92 period and from this extract a pseudo Z score transformation for 1896. The Z score discussed in the statistical literature is a measure which standardizes scores derived from different means. It is derived by dividing the deviation of a given score from the mean by the standard deviation of the entire sample. The variant proposed here is called a pseudo Z score because it is organized across time rather than across space, and because it measures the deviation of a temporal score from the mean established for a series of elections held immediately *before* the one in which the deviation occurs. The assumption is, of course, that an 1896 Democratic deviation of -10.0 from the 1876–92 mean would be more "significant" so far as the relative impact of realignment is concerned in a county with extremely stable pre-existing patterns (say, with a standard deviation for 1876–92 of 1.00) than in one with an identical mean but with far more electoral volatility (for example, a standard deviation of 5.00).[9]

As Map 3.1 reveals, when such transformations are per-

[9] The word "significant" is placed in quotation marks to discourage attacks by methodological purists. This kind of measure, like most of those used in this study, cannot be said in any formal statistical sense to measure significance. It is descriptive only.

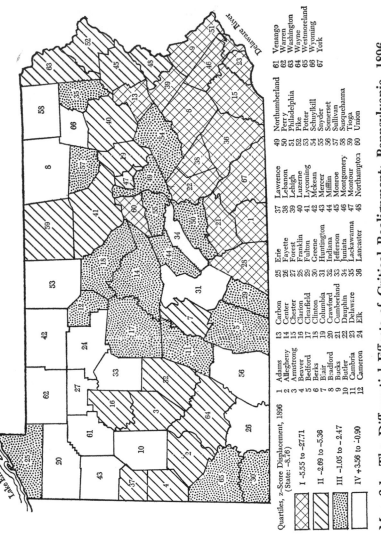

Map 3.1 The Differential Effects of Critical Realignment: Pennsylvania, 1896

formed for the state's sixty-seven counties a remarkably clear-cut regional pattern emerges. Without exception, the most pro-Republican quartile is concentrated in southeastern Pennsylvania, with particularly high and negative county Z scores located in the counties immediately adjacent to the state's largest city. The most pro-Democratic, or perhaps more accurately the least pro-Republican, quartile is found—again, without exception—in rural and semirural counties in areas of the state geographically most remote from major trunk rail lines and metropolitan centers of industry, government, or communications.

In this particular array, urban-rural cleavages as such seem less significant, at least when one moves beyond the area of immediate metropolitan influence, than cleavages involving two polarities. The first of these appears to be ethnicity. Nearly all the counties populated by "old-stock" Pennsylvania Germans, for instance, are in the top pro-Republican quartile of Z scores, while with two exceptions the counties in the bottom quartile had no major concentrations either of Germans or of newer immigrant groups. The second polarization is something that looks very much like a center-periphery cleavage which visibly, if less extremely, corresponds to the 1896 realignment pattern for the country as a whole. Almost all of the bottom-quartile counties were especially remote from the direct influence of transportation or the media of opinion dissemination, which might have spread the northeastern sectional anti-Bryan gospel, as they evidently did in more centrally located parts of the state.

If this were all that was involved in the atypical behavior of these bottom-quartile counties, we might simply suggest an implication of Philip Converse's discussion of information flow and partisan attitudes in the contemporary period.[10] It might be expected, for example, that areas which are remote

[10] Philip E. Converse, "Information Flow and the Stability of Partisan

from centers of opinion dissemination would probably be the least likely to show significant changes in their voting behavior across time; they would tend to be more politically traditionalist than areas fully under metropolitan influence. Indeed, the behavior of the counties in the bottom quartile of pro-Republican movement in 1896 seems to support some such view. Their behavior after 1896, moreover, could be fitted without much difficulty into a model based on a theory of diffusion, since such counties, as we have seen, *subsequently* underwent the strongest secular realignment toward the Republicans of any group in the state.

While such views may be quite suitable to stable phases of the voting cycle, and may also fit the behavior of some areas in critical realignment sequences as well, they are not adequate to the analysis of such sequences as a whole. For example, there is strong evidence that the Republican revolution of the 1850's was especially concentrated in rural areas of New England subculture from Maine to Iowa, and that the larger urban centers even in New England itself tended to resist that redefinition of American politics until 1860–61. Similarly, Key's data for New England in the critical realignment of the 1890's suggest no very marked differences between the voting behavior of the region's cities and its "outback" areas.

We are far as yet from a clear understanding of the motivational bases of such opinion revolutions or their specific distributions. All that can be surmised at this stage is that in 1896 areas of the New England rural-Yankee diaspora from upstate New York westward behaved politically in such a way as to suggest great cross-pressures at work on their voting populations—cross-pressures which may well be related to the transformations in the religious and cultural images of the two major parties which Paul Kleppner has documented for

Attitudes," in Campbell *et al., Elections and the Political Order, op. cit.,* pp. 136–57.

the Midwest during this realigning period.[11] It might be possible, then, to evaluate the 1896 resistance to the Republican tide in such areas as northwest Pennsylvania as a consequence of the cross-pressures between traditionally intense Republican support and the pietistic cultural image reflected in the first Bryan campaign. Similarly, the subsequently heavy secular trend toward the Republican party in such areas might be evaluated as a return to previous partisan commitments consonant with the local subculture, once the short-term influence of Democratic political evangelism in 1896 was removed.

In any event, the evidence seems strong that the political behavior of the ten Pennsylvania counties which were most resistant to the Republican surge in 1896 is closely related to political evangelism before and after that date. Table 3.4 presents an array which differs significantly from the rural-urban array of Table 3.3.

It may first be noted that the ten counties least pro-Republican in 1896 (all of which are geographically concentrated in the extreme northwest) had an even lower Democratic share of the total vote before 1896 than did the metropolitan counties.[12] The sense that this lopsided party balance is connected

[11] Paul Kleppner, *The Cross of Culture* (New York: Free Press, 1970), a treatment of voting alignments in the Midwest from 1850 to 1900 which relies heavily on quantitative analysis. See also one of the earliest studies from this perspective, Lee Benson, *The Concept of Jacksonian Democracy, op. cit.* and, for a discussion of the emergence of Republicanism in Pittsburgh during the 1850's, Michael F. Holt, *Forging a Majority* (New Haven: Yale University Press, 1969). Studies such as these have greatly emphasized the central importance of cultural polarizations based on divergent cultural and religious world views in the shaping of mass voting behavior in the United States, particularly in the nineteenth century. The findings developed here about the Pennsylvania counties most resistant to the statewide Republican surge of the 1890's fit quite neatly into this perspective.

[12] As map 3.1 reveals, the realignment of the 1890's in Pennsylvania was very sharply differentiated geographically. The extremes of Z score displacement are found in the Northwest, where it was minimally pro-Republican, and—with two exceptions—in the far Southeast, where the force of realignment was greatest. The top and bottom ten counties, ranked in terms of the 1896 Z score displacements from the base line of

Table 3.4 Realignment in Pennsylvania: Percentage Democratic of the Total Vote by Categories of 1896 County Z Scores, 1884–1908

Year	10 Least Pro-Republican Counties		45 Intermediate Counties	
	% Dem. of Total	% Prohib. of Total	% Dem. of Total	% Prohib. of Total
1884	38.8	4.2	46.8	1.9
1888	39.4	5.2	47.3	2.4
1892	40.1	5.3	48.3	3.0
1896	41.6	2.9	42.0	2.1
1900	38.0	5.1	42.3	2.8
1904	26.2	9.0	33.0	2.0
1908	33.8	7.7	40.6	1.6

Year	10 Most Pro-Republican Counties		2 Metropolitan Counties	
	% Dem. of Total	% Prohib. of Total	% Dem. of Total	% Prohib. of Total
1884	45.2	1.1	38.5	1.0
1888	44.7	1.8	42.5	0.8
1892	45.4	2.5	41.0	0.9
1896	34.5	1.6	26.2	0.5
1900	36.9	2.3	25.6	1.0
1904	31.5	1.7	17.6	1.1
1908	36.2	2.1	30.0	1.7

percentage Democratic of the two-party vote from 1876 to 1892, are presented below.

County	1896 Z	County	1896 Z
1. Crawford	+3.56	58. Lebanon	− 7.85
2. Venango	+2.16	59. Lehigh	− 7.93
3. Forest	+0.56	60. Dauphin	− 8.33
4. McKean	+0.52	61. Philadelphia	−10.32
5. Bradford	+0.23	62. Union	−11.13
6. Wyoming	−0.18	63. Cumberland	−11.27
7. Warren	−0.36	64. Chester	−13.10
8. Mercer	−0.56	65. Montgomery	−13.64
9. Butler	−0.62	66. Delaware	−16.35
10. Elk	−0.68	67. Bucks	−27.71

with the kind of fundamentalist evangelism which was associated with the "pure" stage of the early Republican Party
coalition is reinforced by the quite abnormal concentration of
Prohibitionist strength throughout the period, except in 1896
itself. Indeed, three aspects of this array suggest that this region was, by Pennsylvania standards at least, a citadel of
radical native-stock protest against the forces shaping modern
industrial America: its very high third-party vote throughout
the period; [13] the very large defection of Democrats in 1904,
ranging beyond even the massive statewide deviation in this
year; and an actual increase in the Democratic percentage of
the total vote in 1896, coupled with a sharp decline in the size
of the third-party protest vote.

In point of fact, there is a good deal of evidence of overlap
between the rural counties which swung most heavily to the
Republican Party in the 1850's and those which were most

[13] Comparing the total third-party presidential vote for the two extreme groups of ten counties each, the percentages are as follows for the
1884–1916 period:

% *"Other" of Total Vote*

Year	10 Counties Least Pro-Republican 1896 Z	10 Counties Most Pro-Republican 1896 Z	Ratio (1)/(2)	State % "Other"
1884	9.3	1.3	7.2	3.6
1888	5.2	1.1	4.7	2.5
1892	8.5	1.7	5.0	3.4
1896	3.0	2.5	1.2	2.7
1900	5.1	1.9	2.7	3.1
1904	11.4	2.3	5.0	4.7
1908	10.1	3.2	3.2	5.7
1912 (except Progressive)	12.5	4.2	3.0	8.5
1916	11.3	2.6	4.4	5.5

With the exception of 1896, when the Gold Democrats inflated the
"other" percentage in the ten bottom counties on the 1896 Z score continuum, the differences between the two sets are systematic and extremely
large.

pro-Democratic or least pro-Republican in the realignment of the 1890's. One may begin by noting that five of the ten counties with the least pro-Republican Z scores in 1896 were also among the ten whose native-stock residents in 1870 had included at least 10 per cent of New York origin. If one carries the time series in Table 3.1 forward from 1884 through 1908, the close similarity of the voting behavior of these ten counties with the lowest pro-Republican ten of 1896 is manifest (see Table 3.5).

The evidence presented here supports two tentative conclusions. In the first place, the massive shifting of the state to

Table 3.5   The Shift from the Third to the Fourth Party System: The Case of Pennsylvania, 1884–1908

Year	10 New York Counties		40 "Other" Counties	
	% Dem. of Total	% Prohib. of Total	% Dem. of Total	% Prohib. of Total
1884	36.9	4.2	46.0	1.9
1888	37.1	5.2	46.3	2.4
1892	38.1	5.0	47.2	3.1
1896	39.2	3.0	40.0	2.2
1900	35.5	5.2	40.3	2.8
1904	23.9	8.3	31.5	3.3
1908	32.1	7.0	38.5	3.3

Year	6 German Counties		2 Metropolitan Counties	
	% Dem. of Total	% Prohib. of Total	% Dem. of Total	% Prohib. of Total
1884	50.9	0.7	38.5	1.0
1888	50.1	1.2	42.5	0.8
1892	51.5	1.7	41.0	0.9
1896	43.0	1.3	26.2	0.5
1900	45.4	1.7	25.6	1.0
1904	39.3	1.6	17.6	1.1
1908	42.9	1.8	30.0	1.7

the Republicans in 1896 was not paralleled by any similar movement in the remote northwestern periphery of the state or in the areas—often overlapping—of transplanted New England settlement. Secondly, both of these overlapping deviant areas underwent a considerably greater-than-average secular trend toward the state's now-dominant Republican coalition after 1896. All of this constitutes one more bit of evidence that party images may have not only been reshuffled but to some extent transposed during the 1890's. Basic to this transposition was the conversion of the Democratic coalition into an explicit vehicle for the defense of colonial interests against those of the metropole, of remote areas against the center in states like Pennsylvania, and of one kind of religiously based political consciousness against another.

The cumulative effect of this realignment and its aftermath was to convert Pennsylvania into a thoroughly one-party state in which basic political issues—within the limits of the politically conceivable of that time, of course—were duly transferred to the Republican primary after it was established in 1908. By the 1920's this peculiar process had been completed. For practical purposes the Democratic Party had become so weakened that, as often as not, the party's nominees for major office were selected by the Republican leadership.[14] Whether so selected or not, their general-election prospects were dismal: of ninety-six statewide contests held from 1893 to 1931, candidates running with Democratic Party endorsement won just one.[15] The political simplicity which had thus matured by the 1920's

[14] Sylvester K. Stevens, *Pennsylvania: Birthplace of a Nation* (New York: Random House, 1964), pp. 270–74.

[15] This involved unusually large scandals within the dominant Republican leadership, and the insurgent candidacy in 1905 of William H. Berry for state treasurer. While he received Democratic support, the large majority of his votes came on another insurgent party line from disgruntled Republicans, and he remained the only insurgent to win state office at a general-election contest with the regular Republican nominee throughout this entire period.

in this industrial heartland of the northeastern metropole was the more extraordinary in an area whose socioeconomic division of labor was as complex and its level of development as high as any in the world. In most other regions of advanced industrialism the emergence of corporate capitalism had been characteristically associated with the development of mass political parties with high structural cohesion and explicit collective, policy- and government-control purposes. It would hardly be an exaggeration to say that the political response to the collectivizing thrust of industrialism in this key American state was the elimination of organized partisan combat, the emergence of a "coalition of the whole" and—by no means coincidentally—a generally highly efficient insulation of the metropole's controlling industrial-financial elite from effective or sustained countervailing pressures from below.[16] Table 3.6, partitioned by decades from the 1860's to the 1960's, indicates some of the quantitative dimensions of this movement.

The reasons for the increasing solidity of this "system of 1896" in Pennsylvania are no doubt complex. Clearly the development of the direct-primary alternative to a general election which no longer had much decisional meaning helped, by destroying the minority party's monopoly of opposition, to undermine the minority party more and more decisively. There is also no doubt that the Republican machines of Pittsburgh and Philadelphia perfected their methods of controlling votes over the first two decades of this century. By 1924, for instance,

---

[16] One notorious instance of this was the establishment of the Coal and Iron Police by the legislature in 1866. In Stevens' words, this was "a privately paid company police system which ruled not only on mine and mill property but the company towns as well. Here they were the only law and order. Tales of their brutalities and invasion of personal rights and liberties of the workers in these towns rival those of the Cossacks of Russia or Hitler's Gestapo. Some five thousand coal and iron police were employed by mining and steel corporations by 1900." (Stevens, *op. cit.*, p. 226.) This piquant example of feudalism was abolished under Pennsylvania's "little New Deal" in 1935.

the Vare-Penrose machine was able to produce a plurality of
293,244 for the Republican presidential ticket in Philadelphia,
which amounted to about 30 per cent of the statewide plurality.[17] These twin steamrollers were enormously effective in
beating back Democratic and progressive Republican challenges at general elections between 1898 and 1910, and remained impressive political forces in the Republican primaries
of the 1918–30 period.

Table 3.6   Pennsylvania, 1864–1968: The Effects of
Periodic Political Realignment

Period	Num-ber of State Offices	Dem. Wins	Mean % Dem. of Total Vote	Vari-ance	Stan-dard Devi-ation	Mean % Rep. of Total Vote	Vari-ance	Stan-dard Devi-ation	Mean % All "Other"	Mean % Dem. of State H.R.
1863–1872	16	1	47.7	7.77	2.79	52.3	7.77	2.79	0.0	39.3
1873–1882	24	9	46.5	8.07	2.84	47.0	11.76	3.43	6.5	44.7
1883–1892	24	1	45.6	2.26	1.50	51.4	1.46	1.20	3.0	33.5
1893–1902	29	0	37.8	9.44	3.07	57.2	14.31	3.78	5.0	22.7
1903–1910	17	1	30.0	66.66	8.16	54.0	65.51	8.09	16.0	17.9
1912–1921	23	0	31.4	23.21	4.82	57.8	35.34	5.94	10.8	17.2
1922–1930	26	0	28.7	41.23	6.42	66.0	52.70	7.26	5.3	10.6
1932–1940	21	12	49.0	22.74	4.77	48.6	15.70	3.97	2.4	52.4
1942–1950	25	6	46.5	11.04	3.32	52.7	10.37	3.22	0.8	37.6
1952–1960	24	12	49.4	5.93	2.43	50.3	6.28	2.51	0.3	48.7
1962–1968	19	10	50.9	25.32	5.03	48.0	23.85	4.88	1.1	51.3

As important as this was, however, it can be argued on a
more basic level that as a rule the Democratic Party after the

[17] One well-known evidence of the total machine domination of Philadelphia voting behavior in this period—especially in the downtown wards
—was the repeated occurrence of a vote of zero at the election-district
level for the machine's opponents (whether Democratic, as in the 1926
senatorial election, or Republican, as in the 1930 gubernatorial election).
The number of divisions in which 100 per cent machine voting occurred
ranged from twelve to twenty-nine during the 1920–30 period, despite a
provision in the state election law which required at least one of the division's election judges to be a member of the minority party.

1890's became largely invisible to Pennsylvania voters as a usable opposition. The machine-generated "insurance" pluralities were not always needed in this period, after all; when they were, the attack came almost always from insurgent Republicans with strong suburban and outstate appeal, not from Democrats. Clearly the national reorganization of parties in and after the 1890's was a dominant cause for the disappearance of the local Democratic Party as a visible general-election alternative. Essentially, the reorganization of the Democratic Party during the Bryan era made it to a very large degree the vehicle of colonial, periphery-oriented dissent against the industrial-metropole center. It was also the vehicle through which the myriad island communities surviving from the nineteenth century sought on occasion to ward off absorption into the larger society being brought into existence under the auspices of industrial capitalism.[18]

But nationally, if not locally, the two-party system not only survived the 1890's but continued to dominate the electoral-politics arena. What we find here is a parodox which pervades American political history. The party system is of preindustrial origin in the United States, and mass political mobilization correspondingly emerged here at an extremely early date. Granted the ethnic heterogeneity and extremely rudimentary political socialization of much of the metropole's working class at the turn of the century, the mainstream of "radical" protest at that time was associated with the neo-Jacksonian political demands of agrarian and small-town social strata which were already obsolescent. The United States was so vast that it had little need of economic "colonies" abroad, since it had two major colonial regions within its own borders. The only kinds

[18] Cf. Samuel P. Hays, "Political Parties and the Community-Society Continuum," in Chambers and Burnham, *op. cit.*, pp. 152–81, and Kleppner, *op. cit.* This also tends to be the argument of David Burner, *The Politics of Provincialism* (New York: Alfred A. Knopf, 1968), although he expands it to include the "urban provincialism" of Al Smith's following.

of attacks which could be made nationally against the emergent industrial "commanding heights"—the only attacks which,
granted the social structure of the country at that time, could
come within striking distance of a popular majority—came out
of these colonial areas. The Democratic Party from 1896 to
1932, and even later, was the national vehicle for these sectional struggles.

The net effect of this was to produce a condition in which—
especially but not entirely on the presidential level—the more
economically advanced a state was the more heavy were its
normal Republican majorities likely to be. The nostalgic
agrarian-individualist colonial appeals of the national Democratic leadership tended to present the voters of metropole
states with the choice between an essentially backward-looking
provincial party articulating an interest opposition to the industrial metropole as a whole and a "modernizing" party based
upon enthusiastic acceptance of and cooperation with the
dominant economic interests of that region and of the country
as a whole. This partitioning of the political universe, of course,
helped to insure crushing Republican majorities in an economically advanced state like Pennsylvania. Moreover, the
survival of national two-party competition on such a basis
helped to insure that no local reorganization of electoral politics along class-stratified lines would be likely to occur even
in such a state. This electoral-politics system thus had enormous built-in stability once it was created and perfected. It
can be surmised that nothing less disruptive than the post-1929
collapse of the national economic system would have been able
to dislodge it.

But it was dislodged. There is an extremely sharp post-1929
break in the Pennsylvania data with the preceding structure of
electoral politics. Our discrepancy-coefficient analysis pinpoints
this at midpoint year 1931, and it was surely well on the way
to completion no later than 1934. While there have been fur-

ther, and rather extensive, readjustments of aggregate voting behavior in this state since the mid-1930's, the structure of major-party alignment remains today quite largely what it was thirty years ago.

Table 3.7 Stages of Realignment in Pennsylvania: Correlations of County Partisan Percentages, 1916–1940, with Rurality and Religion

		Partial Correlations		
Year	Partisan % of Vote	% Catholic 1926	% Rural-Farm 1930	R^2
1916	Democratic (2-party)	−.171	+.161	.036
1920	Democratic (2-party)	−.135	+.109	.020
1924	Democratic (3-party)	−.345	+.376	.169
1924	Progressive (3-party)	+.618	−.525	.433
1928	Democratic (2 party)	+.806	−.386	.654
1932	Democratic (2-party)	−.123	+.008	.015
1936	Democratic (2-party)	+.351	−.541	.297
1940	Democratic (2-party)	+.351	−.506	.264
1920– 1940	Democratic Shift (regression line)	+.517	−.658	.469

Not surprisingly, this upheaval had its premonitory stages, the La Follette Progressive movement of 1924 and Al Smith's candidacy in 1928. Table 3.7 suggests something of the importance of those parties and elections in the process of transition. The residual strength of the Democratic Party toward the end of the fourth party system was diffused in such a way as to show very little correlation with the two variables presented above. There is some evidence for 1916 and 1920 of a continuation of the faintly rural bias of the post-1896 Democratic coalition, and this bias becomes relatively quite conspicuous with the 1924 candidacy of John W. Davis. Quite different relationships emerge when religion and rurality are correlated with the Progressive vote in 1924 and the Democratic vote in 1928. These clearly correspond with the 1936 and 1940 Democratic coalitional base, and particularly with the net shift to the Democratic Party between 1920 and 1940 as this is measured along each county's regression line. Both of these two electoral arrays reveal parts of what is to become a much broader New Deal coalition.

It must be emphasized, however, that the existence of these patterns in the 1920's, impressive precursors of the future though they were, in no way *guaranteed* that realignment along these lines was sure to develop. As late as 1931 the structure of local elections in Pennsylvania fully corresponded to the then usual pattern of widely diffused and overwhelming Republican ascendancy punctuated by factional primary battles between progressives and regulars. Moreover, as is quite evident in Table 3.7, the pattern of 1932 corresponds much more closely to that of the Democratic percentages in 1916–24 then to either that of 1928 or those of 1936 and 1940. Two points are evident from this.

First, 1928 was not a realigning election as such in Pennsylvania. It was part of a realigning sequence which could be so identified only after it had been completed. Second, both the national and local patterns of voting behavior in the 1932 election reveal it to be the last of the sequence beginning in 1896 rather than the first of the New Deal generation.[19] The move-

---

[19] Behavioral evidence for this statement is not too difficult to derive despite the absence of scientific surveys in this period. The most vivid case in point is the extremely close approximation to the 1932 final results which was made by the *Literary Digest* poll and its disastrous misfire in 1936. For a recent account of this, see Julian L. Simon, *Basic Research Methods in Social Science* (New York: Random House, 1969), pp. 111–15. It is evident that the great bias of this sample did not produce serious trouble for the pollsters until the electorate's behavior had been substantially reorganized along class lines, and this clearly had not yet happened by 1932.

ments of the 1920's, of course, clearly foreshadowed the shape and focus of the grand coalition put together by Franklin D. Roosevelt; but that coalition did not come into being until business rule had collapsed along with the laissez-faire economy and until Roosevelt and his advisers had made the key decisions which redefined the subject matter of American domestic politics. Without that colossal shock and without a subsequent dynamic leadership which attempted to cope with its consequences, who can say how, or indeed whether, the system of 1896 would have come to an end?

Table 3.8 Continuity and Change in Pennsylvania:
Correlations of Party Percentages by County, 1916–1940

		Democratic			Progressive
		1916	*1920*	*1924*	*1924*
1916	Democratic	1.000	+.867	+.884	−.151
1920	Democratic	+.867	1.000	+.883	−.275
1924	Democratic	+.884	+.883	1.000	−.397
1924	Progressive	−.151	−.275	−.397	1.000
1928	Democratic	+.235	+.263	+.057	+.498
1932	Democratic	+.648	+.671	+.551	+.287
1936	Democratic	+.424	+.510	+.264	+.241
1940	Democratic	+.400	+.551	+.376	+.291

		Democratic			
		1928	*1932*	*1936*	*1940*
1916	Democratic	+.235	+.648	+.424	+.400
1920	Democratic	+.263	+.671	+.510	+.551
1924	Democratic	+.057	+.551	+.264	+.376
1924	Progressive	+.498	+.287	+.241	+.291
1928	Democratic	1.000	+.680	+.601	+.564
1932	Democratic	+.680	1.000	+.780	+.752
1936	Democratic	+.601	+.780	1.000	+.960
1940	Democratic	+.564	+.752	+.960	1.000

The realignment which terminated the fourth era in our electoral politics was accordingly much more complex and drawn out than was that of the 1890's. Table 3.8 provides a slightly different perspective on this through zero-order correlations among the partisan percentages for the 1916–40 period.

There are two clusters of intercorrelation in excess of +.80— the three Democratic percentages of 1916, 1920, and 1924, on one hand, and the two Democratic percentages of 1936 and 1940, on the other. The 1932 percentage is somewhat more closely related to the two succeeding elections than to any before it, but its moderately high correlation with all Democratic percentages in this period once again indicates its "bridge" character. Otherwise there is a large temporal gap from 1924 to 1936 in which correlations of contiguous elections yield comparatively very low coefficients. The 1928 election, of course, correlates far more strongly with elections after than before it, as its position as a harbinger of realignment would lead us to expect. Finally, the reversal of partisan polarities within the state revealed in Table 3.7 is also evident here: the relationship between the 1940 Democratic percentages and those of any year before 1932 is quite low, with the lowest being 1924 and 1916. The data in these tables make it quite clear that in strong contrast to the realignment of the 1890's, this whole period from 1924 on reveals heavy *within-state* reshuffling of voting behavior. Granted the sectional structuring of the first realignment and the class-ethnic polarization which dominated the second, this difference is entirely to be expected.[20]

It is, of course, important to recognize that realignments constitute not only significant breaking points in an ongoing

[20] This, of course, is exactly what Key found to be the case in his study of New England voting behavior after 1888. Towns with radically differing social structures moved together toward the Republicans in 1896 but showed a profound divergence after 1920, which became very sharp in 1928 and remained stable thereafter. Key, *op. cit.*

process of electoral flow, but that they are also stages in that process. Two chief points about the aftermath of the realignments of the 1930's in Pennsylvania can be made. In the first place, even into the 1960's elections continued to be structured to a considerable extent in terms of the polarizations laid down thirty years before. In other words, the Republican electoral base has remained in the familiar pattern established in the 1930's: native-stock elements living in rural areas, small towns, and suburbs; people with advantages of wealth and education; and people of "obsolescent" social strata, particularly those of traditionalist socioreligious perspectives who tend to resist changes which seem to threaten their traditions. The Democratic electoral base has included disproportionate support among the electorally active poor, Negroes, Jews, Catholics, trade-unionists, and residents of the central city in metropolitan areas. This well-known coalitional structure has remained quite durable in Pennsylvania. If one computes county mean percentages Democratic for the 1932–40 and 1960–68 periods, for example, a correlation of +.757 between the two means is obtained. This is quite high, especially in view of the great span of time between them. A review of multiple correlations of the Democratic percentage of the vote for the 1960–68 period with certain most recent census data (Table 3.9) demonstrates this continuity down to the present time.[21]

While a certain internal shifting among the independent variables correlated with the 1960 and 1968 Democratic percentages can be seen in Table 3.9, the continuity of the pattern after the significant but short-lived compression of polarization in 1964 is evident, particularly when the growing temporal distance between the 1960 data and the most recent election is borne in mind.

The second major point to be made about this contemporary

[21] The data in Table 3.9 are based on data which receive more detailed treatment in Walter Dean Burnham and John D. Sprague, *op. cit.*

Table 3.9 Continuity of Electoral Coalitions in
Pennsylvania, 1960–1968

Partial Correlations: Party Percentages

Variables (1960)	Dem. 1960	Dem. 1964	Dem. 1968	Rep. 1968	Am. Ind. 1968
% Foreign Parents	+.741	+.315	+.563	−.471	−.256
% Nonwhite	+.509	+.023	+.187	−.342	+.079
% Democratic Registration	+.674	+.605	+.561	−.618	+.136
% Rural Farm	−.381	−.521	−.528	+.502	−.112
% High School Graduates	−.424	−.074	−.252	+.213	+.139
R^2	.883	.724	.802	.797	.069

mass structure of electoral politics in Pennsylvania is that
secular trends have been under way which reflect a kind of
"perfection" or "purification" of the orginial patterns brought
into dominance by the electoral politics of the New Deal era.
The basic thrust of change has propelled the Republican Party
into an increasingly clear-cut role—sometimes quixotically performed, as in 1964—as protector of traditional interests and
cultural values against tradition-undermining change, of local
interests against cosmopolitan ones, of peripherally oriented
regional and sectional interests against the aggrandizements
of the dominant, center-oriented Democratic coalition, and
above all as protector of the historic dominance of the private
over the public sectors in society and economy. In this process
states such as Pennsylvania (especially since the subrealign-
ment of 1949–51 which was concentrated in the huge electorate of Philadelphia) have shown both an absolute and a relative secular drift toward the Democrats. This movement has
been particularly evident in presidential-election years.[22]

[22] Walter Dean Burnham, "American Voting Behavior and the 1964
Election," 12 *Midwest Journal of Political Science*, pp. 1–40 (1968).

This secular realignment has involved a fairly unidirectional movement toward heightened polarization along lines foreshadowed by the realigning movements of the 1930's. A correlation of the net Democratic shift between the two means of 1932–40 and 1960–68 with the mean percentage Democratic for 1876–92 yields an r of —.474, suggesting a continuing rotation of this universe toward something approaching a hundred and eighty degrees from its pre-1896 aggregate characteristics. Further reinforcement for the view that center-periphery polarization is continuing to evolve is found by correlating the Democratic shift between the two means with both the 1960 county percentages of "urban" dwellers and the proportion of the population who are members of Protestant denominations with a strongly traditionalist (and very often German) culture.[23] The partial correlation between the Democratic shift and percentage urban is +.318, while it is —.613 between that shift and the percentage of the population belonging to these denominations.[24] In a curious way, such polarizations within this state have paralleled those of the southern region as a whole vis-à-vis national politics as well as those discussed in John Fenton's works on electoral politics in the Midwest and the border states.[25]

Perhaps the most significant general finding which emerges from this discussion is that in Pennsylvania, as in the nation, critical realignments have been both rare and periodic events. It also seems evident on the face of the material examined here that the vast intensification of the state's normal Republican majority occasioned by the realignment of the 1890's corresponds nonetheless to the effects of a critical-realignment sequence despite its abrupt acceleration of a longer-term trend

[23] See Note 3 to Chapter III, above.

[24] $R^2 = .488$. It is also worthy of note that the partial correlation between percentage urban and percentage "traditionalist" is a very low +.028.

[25] John H. Fenton, *Politics in the Border States, op. cit.;* and, by the same author, *Midwest Politics, op. cit.,* especially pp. 219–31.

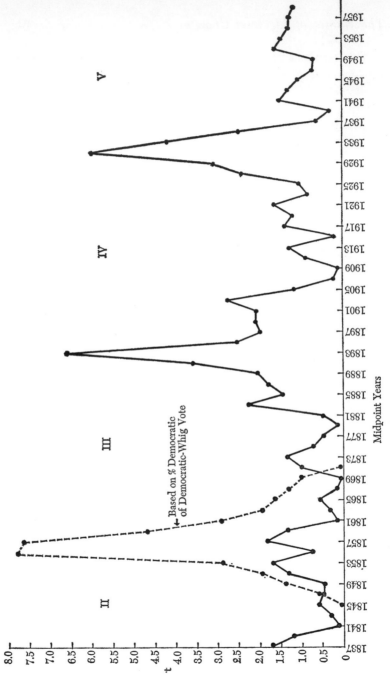

Chart 3.1 Patterns of Stability and Realignment: Pennsylvania, 1828–1968

toward the party which was already dominant in the state's politics. Chart 3.1 provides t values for Pennsylvania for the time span 1828–1968; the state's "political seismicity" stands out in particularly bold relief.[26]

Data for Chart 3.1 The Periodicity of Critical Realignments: The Case of Pennsylvania 1828–1968

Election Sequence	Midpoint Year	M_1	M_2	t	t *
1828–1847	1837	57.1	51.9	1.738	
1829–1848	1839	54.0	51.5	1.248	
1832–1850	1841	51.9	52.0	0.096	
1835–1852	1843	52.0	51.6	0.299	
1836–1854	1845	51.5	50.5	0.592	0
1838–1856	1847	51.9	50.9	0.497	0.518
1840–1858	1849	51.5	50.4	0.483	1.344
1842–1860	1851	52.0	48.8	1.323	1.915
1844–1862	1853	51.6	48.0	1.680	2.890
1846–1864	1855	50.5	48.7	0.737	7.797
1848–1866	1857	50.9	47.3	1.842	7.649
1850–1868	1859	50.4	47.6	1.322	4.683
1852–1870	1861	48.8	48.5	0.134	2.894
1854–1872	1863	48.0	47.3	0.287	1.925
1856–1874	1865	48.7	47.5	0.538	1.648
1858–1876	1867	47.3	47.5	0.146	1.264
1860–1878	1869	47.6	47.6	0.027	1.000
1862–1880	1871	48.5	47.3	0.981	0
1864–1882	1873	47.3	49.3	1.343	
1866–1884	1875	47.5	48.6	0.674	

[26] These t scores are based on *biennial* ten-election sequences. For the period 1828–72, the basic measure is the percentage Democratic of the total vote for the leading office in each election year (gubernatorial rather than presidential in 1860 and 1872). For the period 1875–1968, the basic measure is the mean percentage Democratic of the total vote for all offices in a given election in which the state is the elective unit. The r_d^2 scores, not given here, are virtually identical with the t scores in their relative magnitude.

Data for Chart 3.1 The Periodicity of Critical
Realignments: The Case of Pennsylvania 1828–1968 (*Cont.*)

Election Sequence	Midpoint Year	M_1	M_2	t	t^*
1868–1886	1877	47.5	48.3	0.445	
1870–1888	1879	47.6	47.8	0.110	
1872–1890	1881	47.3	48.1	0.454	
1874–1892	1883	49.4	46.9	2.224	
1876–1894	1885	48.6	45.2	1.403	
1878–1896	1887	48.3	43.2	1.782	
1880–1898	1889	47.8	42.3	1.962	
1882–1900	1891	48.1	39.9	3.578	
1884–1902	1893	46.9	38.9	6.546	
1886–1904	1895	45.2	37.3	2.515	
1888–1906	1897	43.2	36.1	1.940	
1890–1908	1899	42.3	35.2	2.065	
1892–1910	1901	39.9	32.7	2.063	
1894–1912	1903	38.9	31.9	2.733	
1896–1914	1905	37.3	33.5	1.160	
1898–1916	1907	36.1	35.4	0.207	
1900–1918	1909	35.2	34.9	0.092	
1902–1920	1911	32.7	35.8	0.889	
1904–1922	1913	31.9	35.7	1.277	
1906–1924	1915	33.5	33.0	0.144	
1908–1926	1917	35.4	30.5	1.345	
1910–1928	1919	34.9	30.6	1.180	
1912–1930	1921	35.8	30.8	1.584	
1914–1932	1923	35.7	32.4	0.791	
1916–1934	1925	33.0	38.2	0.955	
1918–1936	1927	30.5	44.0	2.398	
1920–1938	1929	30.6	46.3	3.086	
1922–1940	1931	30.8	50.7	5.954	
1924–1942	1933	32.4	50.7	4.178	
1926–1944	1935	38.2	50.5	2.466	
1928–1946	1937	44.0	47.2	0.590	
1930–1948	1939	46.3	47.6	0.273	

Election Sequence	Midpoint Year	M_1	M_2	t	t *
1932–1950	1941	50.7	46.7	1.455	
1934–1952	1943	50.7	47.2	1.269	
1936–1954	1945	50.5	47.6	1.001	
1938–1956	1947	47.2	48.8	0.689	
1940–1958	1949	47.6	49.2	0.660	
1942–1960	1951	46.7	49.8	1.612	
1944–1962	1953	47.2	49.9	1.424	
1946–1964	1955	47.6	50.8	1.257	
1948–1966	1957	48.8	51.1	1.243	
1950–1968	1959	49.2	51.3	1.138	

* Based on Democratic percentage of Democratic-Whig vote.

Viewed over the long run since the modern shape of American electoral politics came into existence, the pattern presented by Pennsylvania is clearly one of very great long-term stability extending over decades, followed by intense bursts of electoral reorganization. Within this state at least, only the period of the 1850's, with its very low peaking of t, seems anomalous. Some of the underlying causes of this peculiarity have already been discussed in this chapter. Essentially the reorganization of American politics during this period was very much a question of geographical latitude in the North no less than in the country as a whole. Pennsylvania, like other middle states, lay south of the heartland of the Republican revolution, with the consequence, as we have seen, that the Republicans inherited most of the old Whig following but with very little change otherwise.

At the same time, the basic national characteristic of this realignment was its unparalleled violence, resulting in the destruction of one of the major parties and its replacement by another with a quite different geographical base and orientation to public policy. This is surely a distinction with a difference; and so we provide an alternative measure of t in

Chart 3.1, one based on the Democratic percentage of the two-party Democratic-Whig vote for the period 1838–78. Of course, when this measure is used, the result is that very high t values are generated at the point in time when the Whig percentage of the two-party vote begins to collapse toward zero, and hence a major electoral transition is identified for the midpoint years 1855 and 1857. Thus it is that each measure describes one part of the reality of that time: nationally, the most sweeping political realignment in the country's history, yet a reorganization of politics in Pennsylvania which, while sweeping in its partisan and policy consequences, was fashioned out of electoral shifts occurring in only a few areas of the state.

This exhaustive survey of the electoral politics of a single state over a century suggests a number of aspects of critical realignments which can be restated at this point.

1. There is what might be described as a "normal" pattern of electoral politics which is marked by great internal stability in voting alignments, enduring for considerable periods of time. The precise degree of stability will vary with a complex of characteristics associated with the electoral era being studied. Thus, for instance, variances in mean party percentages were much larger in the 1900–30 period than in the periods before and after.[27] Each of these eras was, nevertheless, relatively highly stable in partisan terms. The 1858–93 period was one of narrow but usually decisive Republican dominance in a highly competitive partisan context; the 1894–1932 period was one of heavy and increasing Republican ascendancy under thoroughly one-party conditions; and the 1934–68 period was one of intense and usually close partisan competition with coalitional patterns which were forged in the 1930's.

2. This pattern of inertial stability is only part of a larger dynamic or dialectical process: it is periodically and quite

[27] See Table 3.6, p. 52 in text.

abruptly shattered by sudden, major reorganizations of mass voting behavior in which high levels of sociopolitical tension are closely associated with abnormally intense political conflict at all stages, often preceded by third-party uprisings against the existing major parties and followed by "abnormal" mass movements—mobilization of hitherto inactive strata in the potential electorate and the movement of decisively large minorities of already active voters from one major-party commitment to another. Realigning elections are clearly qualitatively different from the norm of American electoral politics; their patent issue orientation, their capacity to transform and to mobilize at the mass base, and their constituent, *decisive* character suggest as much. These fundamental qualitative differences also suggest that models of voting behavior derived from the normal inertial stability of a mass middle-class identified electorate, which usually has no felt need to consume much political information and no great perceived personal stake in the outcome, may fall short of describing the total potentialities of the American voter when abnormal circumstances politicize him.

3. The timing of this disruption of the normal inertia of American voting behavior can be determined quantitatively with considerable precision. In the case of Pennsylvania, although by no means everywhere, discontinuities tend to appear at the same time as they do nationally. There have been three realigning cycles in the state since the organization of "modern" party politics in the 1830's; the midpoints are 1855/1857, 1893, and 1931. There have been in addition intermediate points of electoral transition which may be described as "subrealigning," indicating a good deal of politically related stress in the electorate but not enough to produce sweeping transformations of the voting universe as a whole. In Pennsylvania these fall at midpoints 1873, 1911 and 1913, and 1951—that is, about halfway in the course of the so-called "stable phase" which

stretches from one realignment to the next. Clearly these major disruptions in electoral politics are in direct temporal relationship with crises profoundly affecting the entire national socioeconomic structure and—whatever the numerology of the case may be—such crises have recurred one long generation apart for more than a century.

4. Each realignment was in effect a set of constituent decisions by critical minorities within the electorate and by elites working within the majorities brought into being by critical elections. These decisions reallocated the processes and outputs of politics in terms of the interests of major elements in the new coalition and, in one form or another, served to manage and contain the political tensions which contributed to realignment. In the case of Pennsylvania, for instance, the net effects of the realignments of the 1850's seem to have involved the replacement of one set of "machine" leaders by another. The latter leaders provided indispensable support for the Union effort in the Civil War, as the leaders of the Pennsylvania Democratic Party might well not have done. They were also more unambiguously related to the emergent leaders of industrial capitalism than were the Democrats who dominated the state during the second party system. The 1890's immeasurably solidified the ascendancy of the Republican-industrialist political complex, in Pennsylvania even more completely than in the nation at large. Finally, the realignment of the 1930's may be viewed as involving the development of structures of countervailing power—or a vast pluralization of politics—through the unionization of labor in the coal and steel industries, the ending of the grossest forms of company-town feudalism, and the mobilization of new immigrants and their children into a reconstituted Democratic Party.

5. It would seem clear enough that each realignment has been followed by a major "party system" or, if one will, that there have been a number of quite discrete eras of American

electoral politics. Each differs in quite fundamental matters of style and substance from its predecessors and successors. To restate one obvious case in point: party competition, which existed under conditions of very full mobilization during the third system, was brought substantially to an end under conditions of "electoral demobilization" during the fourth. When it was restored in the fifth era, the bases of that competition were as fundamentally transformed from those of the nineteenth century as were the nature and scope of governmental policy-making. One generalization which has firm footing in this analysis of a single state's electoral politics is that the label of the bottle and its contents are two quite different things. It is true, of course, that the same two major parties have largely monopolized the American political arena since 1860. It is also true that the shifts in party coalitions have never become total at any one time during this period, even under the great pressures of critical realignments. But the case of Pennsylvania forcefully suggests how little the Democratic coalitions of, say, 1884, 1924, and 1968 have in common with each other.

When the phenomenon of critical realignment is placed at the center of our thinking about American politics, we also confront the existence of long periods in which political coalitions forged during preceding realignment sequences endure with only limited change. Such durable coalitions help to define what the agenda of politics is about in any given period. Of course, there are real dangers that we may oversimplify a complex reality by forcing it into a rigidly compartmentalized scheme. At the same time, we may conclude from accumulating empirical evidence that there have been five electoral eras or "party systems" of roughly equal duration in the political history of the country. Identification of these eras and of the realigning sequences which separate them may permit us new and interesting ways to think about the dynamics not only of this country's electoral politics but also of its political life as a whole. In particular, we may wish to inquire into the mechanisms by which groups not particularly conspicuous for their influence on politics during one era become mobilized in the next or, conversely, how and why it is that groups which are effectively mobilized into the voting system in one era are demobilized or even expelled in the next. We may also be made sensitive to questions which involve the relationship between phenomena—and particularly changes—which have hitherto been viewed separately, if they have been perceived at all, in the existing literature on American politics. Above all, we may find it important to attempt hypotheses as to the origins of the peculiar dynamic relationship between "party system" and critical realignment. The next chapters are devoted to these tasks.

4

The Movement Toward Depoliticization: The "System of 1896" and the American Electorate

Before turning to a discussion of the etiology of critical realignment and its relation to the American political system, it is necessary to examine in detail not only the periodic recurrence of realignment, but undirectional, post-1900 trends toward the degeneration of party linkages in our system of electoral politics. This discussion falls analytically into two parts. The first of these involves analysis of some of the ways in which rules of the game were changed during and after the great industrialist breakthrough of the 1890's, as well as their interaction with a massive and largely permanent transformation in aggregate electoral behavior which originated in this period. The second, the contemporary trend toward "electoral disaggregation," will be discussed in the next chapter.

Electoral politics in the last part of the nineteenth century was marked by a number of features which differentiate it sharply from the post-1920 variant. Most of these features were derived from the structure of politics which had been constructed during the second party system, in a largely rural political economy undergoing the first major push toward industrialization and urbanization. They included such features as party-activist control of nominations and platforms through the convention; partisan printing and distribution of ballots or "tickets" to voters on—and sometimes before—election day; large numbers of elective offices at all levels, and partisan patronage control of most appointive ones; and an extremely full mobilization of the potential electorate which was closely related to the intensity and rigidity of party competition.

The political style of this period has been described in a recent paper by Richard Jensen as "militarist." [1] The images were those of armies drawn up for combat, and financial and communications "sinews of war" were provided by an elaborate, well-staffed, and strongly motivated organizational structure. In the field of communications, a partisan popular press was dominant—a phenomenon very much evident in Norwegian party politics at present but which has become extinct here since the turn of the century. [2] The "drilling" of voters in this period by their party captains was intense, and presupposed both highly stable partisan commitments in the mass

[1] Richard Jensen, "American Election Campaigns: A Theoretical and Historical Typology (paper delivered at the 1968 convention of the Midwest Political Science Association), especially pp. 2–10.

[2] See, for example, Angus Campbell and Henry Valen, "Party Identification in Norway and the United States," in Campbell *et al., Elections and the Political Order, op. cit.,* pp. 245–68; and especially Henry Valen and Daniel Katz, *Political Parties in Norway* (Oslo: Universitetsforlaget, 1964), pp. 35–56. Of 194 newspapers in Norway in 1957, 150 (77.3 per cent) were supporters of one of the political parties or antagonistic to socialism and the Labor Party.

electorate and a parallel cultural pattern of intense participation extending quite beyond even the very large turnout percentages of the era. It is estimated, for instance, that 750,000 persons from all over the country visited McKinley's home during the "Front Porch" campaign of 1896, a figure which amounts to about 5 per cent of the total vote and 13 per cent of the Republican vote in November! [3] Nor were such monster outpourings as the Sound Money parade in New York in that year less remarkable indicators of the extent of mass effort.

It is worth noting to what a large extent the then existing structure of voting behavior—under the rules of the game at the time, of course—shaped the strategic considerations of partisan elites. Little was to be gained by attempting to convert a large "floating" or independent vote, for the good reason that almost none existed. In this period there was no popular cultural support for the "independent" voter as the man who evaluated candidates and issues on the merits and arrived at an informed decision. On the contrary, such people tended to be scorned as "traitors," "turncoats," or corrupt sellers of their votes. Thus rational party strategy and compaign tactics were overwhelmingly oriented to the "drill" and to the mobilization of the maximum possible number of known party followers at the polls. In such a context the purchase of votes also became a rational strategy. If the Republicans in part "bought" the election of 1888 by paying a five-dollar gold piece to each of some thousands of purchased and imported voters in Indiana, this was possible short of bankruptcy because rather narrow limits were fixed by the thoroughly mobilized and closely balanced "committed" electorate.[4] What party leader would make the attempt today in a jurisdiction as large and volatile as a state?

[3] Jensen, "American Election Campaigns," *op. cit.*, pp. 17–18.
[4] Compare the Indiana electoral data—particularly for the period before 1894—in Table 1 in the Appendix.

The transition from this state of affairs was, in large measure, what the political side of progressive-era reform was all about. Not only the foreign observer Ostrogorski,[5] but many of the "best men" associated with progressivism and deeply imbued with traditional old-stock American middle-class values (individualism, anticorruptionism, nativism, and antiurbanism) came to regard the ascendancy of party organizations and the rigidity of mass voting behavior as the enemy to be attacked. Much of the agitation for such reforms as direct election of senators, the direct primary, the initiative, and women's suffrage was couched in a doubtless sincere democratic-egalitarian rhetoric. Some was not, as for example in the justifications used for deliberate malapportionment in the New York constitutional convention of 1894 or for the various measures employed to eliminate Negro voting in the South between 1890 and 1904. But most if not all of these fundamental changes in the "rules of the game" were in effect devices of political stabilization and control, with strongly conservative latent consequences if not overt justifications, and with an overwhelming antipartisan bias.

The reform of American electoral politics which took place in and after the 1890's can be subdivided into several generally complementary parts.

1. *The Erosion of Functions Performed by Political Parties.* The first of these reforms was the introduction of the Australian ballot, begun on a statewide basis with Massachusetts in 1889 and largely completed by the end of the 1890's. This reform—which was supposed to purify elections of corruption and intimidation but of course did not in a number of notoriously machine-controlled jurisdictions—stripped from the parties a major organizational function: the printing and distribution

[5] M. Ostrogorski, *Democracy and the Organization of Political Parties,* Vol. II (New York: Macmillan, 1902).

of ballots.[6] It was also associated in a number of states with the adoption of an office-block ballot form, which made voting a straight ticket much more complicated and confusing than it had been.

The second reform was the adoption of the direct-primary system, concentrated in the years 1903–13 and adopted by all but a few states by the 1920's. The literature dealing with the consequences of primaries—particularly when they become substitutes for general-election competition in one-party states —is by now voluminous and needs no further exposition here.[7] Clearly a tremendous impetus for the adoption of this organization-undermining reform was the post-1896 conversion of most parts of the United States into one-party bailiwicks, with the consequent erosion of significant choice at the general election. There seems little question that, on the whole, adoption of the direct primary served by an interactive process to reinforce one-partyism by stripping the minority party of its sole remaining resource, monopoly of opposition.[8]

The progressive era also witnessed a major assault led largely by the "best people" in local elite and middle-class positions against the evils of the urban machine. As Samuel

[6] This was quite accurately perceived by some party leaders, particularly those, like Governor David B. Hill of New York, who had been thoroughly socialized politically by the party-loyalty norms of the third party system. He twice vetoed efforts to established the Australian ballot in New York on the grounds that it would tend to undermine both democracy and the organization of political parties. *Public Papers of David B. Hill,* 1889, pp. 12–20, 144–74. For a discussion of this which is conventionally unsympathetic and in the progressive-era tradition, see L. E. Fredman, *The Australian Ballot* (East Lansing, Mich.: Michigan State University Press, 1968), especially pp. 42–45.

[7] As is so often the case in this field, the seminal contribution was made by V. O. Key, Jr., in "The Direct Primary and Party Structure," 48 *American Political Science Review,* pp. 1–26 (1954); and, by the same author, *American State Politics* (New York: Alfred A. Knopf, 1956), pp. 85–196.

[8] *Ibid.,* pp. 194–96.

P. Hays points out, these reforms, imbued with the image of
the successful business corporation as applied to political affairs, were also and necessarily directed against the polyglot of
local interests which had become deeply rooted in a largely
immigrant-oriented community milieu.[9] Successful implementa-
tion of such reforms as at-large elections of city council members, nonpartisan local elections, and the city-manager movement of the 1920's led not only to the erosion of party where
they were carried out but also to heavy curtailment of the
leverage previously exercised in the political arena by the class-
ethnic infrastructure and its representatives.

Although legislation had little if any direct part in it, the
disappearance of the old partisan-oriented press and the rise
of a modern mass journalism which conspicuously prided itself
on being far above mere partisan politics constituted a major
sea change of the period. While the partisan press was not the
only means by which a political organization could communi-
cate with its following, it had been of immense importance
in "spreading the word" and in contributing to the massive
mobilizations characteristic of the third system. Its disappearance signaled not only the partial demise of a critically
important partisan communication function but a basic cultural change in the mass public, which in turn required the
development of entirely new party and candidate strategies
for winning elections.

2. *Manipulation of Voting Qualifications and Requirements.*
A prominent aspect of the period was the rapid spread of
women's suffrage, culminating in the Nineteenth Amendment
(1920). Wyoming had adopted this reform in territorial elections as early as 1869, but the movement did not resume until
Colorado's enfranchisement of 1893. The conventional view of
this movement, until recently, was to accept it on face value
as a democratic, egalitarian reform and so, of course, it was

[9] Hays, *op. cit.,* especially pp. 171–80.

in the obvious sense. But a recent study by Alan Grimes has emphasized other facets: a strongly moralist and nativist flavor and a concentration of support for the reform among middle-class Protestants who were often deeply antagonistic to the corrupting influences of the polyglot metropolis.[10]

It is, of course, highly unlikely that many reformers perceived clearly that women's suffrage would in the short run dilute the political power of the immigrants because of widespread cultural traditions among the latter that discouraged female participation in politics. Such was, however, the demonstable effect, particularly before the 1928 election.[11] Significantly, the movement spread first from west to east: from a colonial area of the country with relatively few "newer immigrants," a relative scarcity of women, strong moralist subcultural traditions, and a post-1900 stronghold of a political progressivism which had exceptionally pronounced antipartisan overtones.

Without much question, the most notable and fateful manipulation of the electorate occurred in the eleven ex-Confederate states once it had become clear after the failure of the Force Bill of 1891 and the partial repeal of Reconstruction

[10] Alan P. Grimes, *The Puritan Ethic and Woman Suffrage* (New York: Oxford University Press, 1967). It was characteristic of the mobilization politics practiced during the nineteenth century that a large number of states, particularly in the Midwest and the West, permitted aliens to vote if they had declared their intention to become citizens. It is equally characteristic of the 1890–1920 period that alien suffrage was abolished. The last states to retain it were Indiana (until 1921) and Arkansas (until the mid-1920's).

[11] See H. L. A. Tingsten, *Political Behavior* (London: King, 1937), pp. 30–33. Particularly suggestive is the massive differential in male-female turnout rates during the 1920's in Chicago, an ethnically polyglot metropolis with many recent immigrants, and Delaware, Ohio, a small town of overwhelmingly native-stock Protestant population. The first in 1920 showed a male turnout of 75 per cent and a female turnout of 46 per cent, a differential of 29 per cent; the second in 1924 showed turnouts of 73 per cent and 57 per cent respectively, a differential of only 16 per cent.

statutes in 1894 that the federal government was no longer
seriously interested in the conduct of southern elections. The
precise timing of this movement can be pinpointed; it began
in Florida and Mississippi in 1890, proceeded through the
South Carolina convention of 1895, the North Carolina *"coup
d'état"* of 1898, and the Alabama and Virginia disfranchise-
ments of 1901–2, and was completed in Texas in 1904. The
literature of the devices by which southern electorates were
reduced to small fractions of their former size is voluminous
and well known, as are the devices themselves: the poll tax,
the excessively long residence requirement, the discriminatory
literacy test, and, of course, a whole host of extralegal control
measures.[12]

A very recent treatment of this movement for one (not
necessarily typical) southern state may, however, be mentioned
here: Raymond H. Pulley's *Old Virginia Restored.*[13] Drawing
on insights from such revisionist historians as Robert Wiebe
and Samuel P. Hays, Pulley makes an impressive case for the
interpretation of disfranchisement and the solidification of one-
party supremacy in Virginia as part of a *progressive* impulse
toward control and management of a dangerously volatile
colonial electorate. In this case, as he argues, the image was, of
course, one of restoration of an hypostasized "Old Virginia"
dominated by an elite filled with noblesse oblige and far removed from the corruption and turmoil of fully democratic
politics. In view of the spectacularly radical proclivities of its
white rural electorate as revealed in the traumatic Readjuster
episode of the 1880's, its economically colonial status after the
Civil War, and its ever-present "Negro problem"—progressivism and "good government" could only come about in
Virginia through the substantial liquidation of political de-

----

[12] An excellent and rather early study of this is Paul Lewinson, *Race,
Class and Party* (original ed., 1932; New York: Grosset & Dunlap, 1965).
[13] Charlottesville: The University of Virginia Press, 1968.

mocracy. It might be useful here to indicate precisely how effective this set of controls came to be by examining turnout and party competition in Virginia presidential and gubernatorial elections since 1869 (Table 4.1).[14]

This may seem an extreme example of the effectiveness of massed electorate-control measures during—indeed, well after —the fourth national voting system; if so, it was frequently paralleled elsewhere in this period, particularly in the South. If Pulley is correct in his view that the elite impulse to convert democracy into oligarchy was not only specifically Virginian but specifically progressive as well, the case becomes more interesting still. For it may well be argued that Virginia, in dismantling political parties and erecting high legal and customary barriers to political participation at the mass base after 1890, only carried to a local extreme an impulse which profoundly influenced American politics as a whole during those years.

Finally, one finds the development of personal-registration requirements in nearly all states during this period.[15] This change in the rules of the game requires somewhat more extensive discussion, not least because of its role in a dynamic interaction process that is not yet well understood. One may begin by noting that the drive toward registration grew out of the same interrelated complex of impulses toward control and management which we have already discussed. The original impetus to the adoption of personal-registration requirements clearly grew out of that old-stock nativist and corporate-

[14] Turnout in Democratic primaries, of course, was not much higher: between 1905, the first, and 1961—there was no primary opposition for governor in 1965—it fluctuated between a maximum of 17.4 per cent (1905) and a minimum of 6.9 per cent (1957). Turnout estimates are based on linear interpolations between census years and on the potential total electorate. In Virginia, this is the total adult-male citizen population prior to 1920 and the total adult citizen population thereafter.

[15] Except for those which, like Texas and Arkansas, used poll-tax receipts as equivalents.

Table 4.1 Party Voting and Turnout in Virginia, 1869–1969

	Gubernatorial Elections			*Presidential Elections*	
Year	*% Voting of Potential Electorate*	*% Dem.* *	*Year*	*% Voting of Potential Electorate*	*% Dem.* *
1869	84.8	54.3	1872	66.2	49.5
1873	74.9	56.4	1876	77.6	59.6
1877	34.1	100.0	1880	64.1 45.5 +	15.1
1881	63.2	47.2	1884	81.7	51.1
1885	81.9	52.8			
1889	76.8	57.5	1888	83.2	50.3
1893	54.7	61.2	1892	75.3	59.2
1897	40.3	65.9	1896	71.0	53.4
1901	44.5	58.9	1900	59.6	55.8
1905	27.0	64.6	1904	27.7	62.6
1909	22.0	63.7	1908	27.4	61.2
1913	13.4	100.0	1912	25.7	66.7 *
1917	15.6	72.0	1916	27.1	67.6
1921	17.5	66.3	1920	19.4	61.8
1925	11.7	74.1	1924	18.1	62.5 *
1929	21.0	63.0	1928	24.0	46.0
1933	12.1	75.3	1932	22.1	69.5
1937	9.8	84.0	1936	23.0	70.5
1941	7.6	82.0	1940	22.1	68.3
1945	9.5	68.2	1944	22.3	62.5
1949	13.3	72.0	1948	21.6	48.2 *
1953	19.7	55.3	1952	29.9	43.5
1957	23.3	63.4	1956	31.8	40.9
1961	16.8	63.9	1960	33.3	47.2
1965	22.8	48.3 *	1964	42.7	53.7
1969	35.0	46.2	1968	52.9	32.7 *

* Democratic percentage of three-party vote; otherwise, of two-party vote.

minded hostility to the political machine, the polyglot city, and the immigrant which was so important a component of the progressive mentality. Here too there were flagrant abuses which had developed in the "militarist" politics of the nineteenth century as they were modified by industrial-urban development. In large anonymous metropolitan hives the old practice of personally recognizing qualified voters at the polls, which had been effective (and still is) in rural areas and small towns, became an obvious vehicle of political corruption.

Compulsory registration was first required for residents of cities above a certain size, and was only later, if ever, extended to the whole population of a state; this is still the procedure in a number of states, including Ohio and Missouri. In some cases the urge to control the possibly dangerous or subversive potential of mass urban electorates was clearly expressed: thus—verbally—in the 1894 decision to malapportion to protect the "true Americans" of upstate New York from the immigrant masses of New York City, and—statutorily—in the requirement, applicable to New York City alone for many years, that registration not only be personal but periodic.

Stanley Kelley and his associates are surely right in their argument that the imposition of a personal-registration requirement serves to depress voter participation by differentially increasing costs of access.[16] In the present era, for example, the differential in turnout between registration and nonregistration territory in Missouri and Ohio ranges between 10 and 15 per cent. Nor is there any doubt that the differential costs of registration (as well as other variables) are duly revealed in any class-stratification analysis of voter participation. To take one example where fairly detailed contemporary voting and other data are available, one may examine participation and partisan voting in the 1960 election in Baltimore (Table 4.2).

This heavily class-oriented skewing of participation is a

[16] Stanley Kelley *et al.*, "Registration and Voting: Putting First Things First," 61 *American Political Science Review*, pp. 359–79 (1967).

Table 4.2 Class, Party, and Turnout: The Case of
Baltimore, 1960

% Professional-Managerial of Adult Males by Racial Composition, 1960	Number of Political Tracts Analyzed	Mean Turnout	Mean % Democratic of 2-Party Presidential Vote
White (0–49.9% Nonwhite)			
40% and Over	8	70.8	43.9%
20–39.9%	18	62.1	55.0
10–19.9%	14	52.6	61.9
0– 9.9%	14	52.1	71.2
Black (50% + Nonwhite)			
10% and Over	7	51.9	72.3
0– 9.9%	23	41.0	75.1
City as a Whole	84	54.0	63.9

characteristic feature of contemporary American electoral
politics. The extremely high turnout figures which are typical
in the last quarter of the nineteenth century make it very
doubtful that such bias existed in this country prior to 1900 on
anything like the scale it does now. Nor, granting the incentives
of machine politics toward the maximum possible mobilization
of party supporters during the "militarist" era, should this be
greatly surprising. Moreover, as is well known, this class differential in participation is far less visible in most other
present-day Western democracies, particularly in those with
multiparty systems and thorough social organization of the
class infrastructure.

To take an extreme case on this side, electoral participation
in Sweden is both very high and quite invariant along class
lines. Thus, for example, the 1960 Swedish elections to the
lower chamber of the Riksdag revealed a turnout of 88 per
cent among working-class males, with a national cross-class
participation rate of 87.6 per cent, and 91.2 per cent among

female workers, with a national cross-class participation rate among married women of 91.1 per cent.[17] One might anticipate this in a small country with very limited problems of ethnicity, a dominant class structuring of electoral politics, and a well-organized social infrasturcture, but it should be noted that it has a system of electoral law—shared in one form or another with practically all other developed democratic polities—in which the responsibility for compiling electoral registers and keeping them up to date falls on the state, not on the individual.

This, of course, is precisely the point. Kelley's analysis must be regarded as only a beginning in exploring the problems of turnout in the United States. There are several important questions to be asked regarding this singular American electoral rule. Why is it that we have statutes requiring *personal* registration? Why has this device been so widely adopted as to permit few deviations, except of detail, from one state statute to another? Why has it received so little attention, on the whole, from reform-minded political scientists and others interested in democratizing the base of our electoral politics? Finally, what might be the implications of its confinement to urban areas, which was originally very widespread and is still frequently encountered? Merely to ask such questions is to suggest, and rather strongly, that the American peculiarity of personal registration ought not to be received by analysts as a given. It is a phenomenon which has deeply involved electorate-control decisions, even if the involvement has often been implicit and the decisions unconscious because the values on which they were based are so universally shared in the political culture.

In addition, there is the problem of attempting to identify the extent to which the adoption of personal-registration requirements actually affected the steep post-1900 decline in voter participation. The evidence, of course, has to be in-

[17] *Statistisk Årsbok for Sverige,* 1964, p. 380.

ferential or circumstantial rather than direct, but it is cumu-
latively very impressive: while the introduction of personal
registration clearly played some role, the decline in turnout
which occurred after 1896 and *before* the date of women's
suffrage was not only widespread but cut across registration-
territory boundaries. Of course, it was much steeper in some
areas than in others, especially in the South, where the costs
of voting were deliberately made so high by those in charge of
local politics that probably half of the white electorate was
effectively disfranchised along with almost all the Negroes.

But among the thirty-four nonsouthern states participating
in both the 1896 and 1916 elections, only eight showed some
increases in participation; twenty-six showed more or less
severe declines. Five of these states with increases (Nebraska,
Nevada, North Dakota, Utah, and Wyoming) are in the trans-
Mississippi west, where the general effect of the 1896 realignment was to make politics more competitive than it had been
previously; the other three include two in New England
(Maine and Rhode Island), where local factors seem to have
been involved, and Delaware, where competitive politics survived the realignments of the 1890's. On the other hand, most
of the larger industrial states lost 15 to 20 per cent of their
presidential electorates during this period, despite the partisan
upheavals of 1912 and the closeness of the 1916 election. It is
extremely unclear that the introduction of personal registration
at the beginning of the fourth electoral era had more than a
very marginal contributing effect to this outcome, particularly
in such states as Ohio, Indiana, and Kansas, where it was
applicable only in cities of varying minimum sizes. The movement was systemic, and seems to be clearly related to the
disappearance of effective interparty competition throughout
much of the country.

This can be confirmed by a somewhat closer examination.
Between 1906 and 1937 a set of registration statutes was en-

acted by the Pennsylvania legislature which required personal registration in cities, but not in rural areas or small towns.[18] In this respect the "rules of the game" were similar to those adopted at about the same time and still in existence in Missouri and some other states. But unlike Pennsylvania, in Missouri, a border state, the net effect of the realignments of the 1890's was to make the parties more competitive than they had been before 1894 or than they were to be after 1930. Assuming a rough similarity of classes of people covered by personal registration requirements (although not, of course, the relative proportion of each state's electorate so covered), one would anticipate finding considerable differences in turnout regression lines plotted over time. Such differences are very clearly marked, and are indicated in Table 4.3.

The decline in Pennsylvania's turnout along a regression line extending from the 1870's to World War I was precipitate, both in presidential and off-year elections. For Missouri, on the other hand, almost no secular trend is visible in this period. Similarly for the 1920–68 period: Pennsylvania's turnout shows a heavy increase in presidential years and an even more substantial one in off-year gubernatorial contests, revealing a tendency for electoral slack or dropoff in this state to undergo severe secular decline after the onset of the New Deal realignment. Missouri, on the other hand, continues to show very slight secular trend in presidential elections during this period.

What is impressive here is the considerable opening up of electoral slack in off-year elections after 1920, which may be said to have an obvious institutional explanation: in Missouri the major contests affecting state politics are decided in presidential years, in Pennsylvania they are not. Even so, however, one highly visible office—that of U.S. Senator—has come up for election in Missouri in two of every three off-year elections

[18] For the relevant state election statutes and changes in them, see *The Pennsylvania Manual*, 1907–1937.

Table 4.3 Contrasts in Participation, 1874–1968:
The Cases of Missouri and Pennsylvania

Period	$Y_c =$	Net % Change (on regression line)	Dropoff at Beginning	Dropoff at End
Missouri				
1876–1916 (President)	78.81 +0.10 X	+1.3	14.7	17.1
1874–1918 (No major office)	67.56 −0.11 X	−1.8		
1920–1968 (President)	69.27 −0.10 X	−1.9	28.0	37.4
1922–1966 (No major office)	50.52 −0.73 X	−8.0		
Pennsylvania				
1876–1916 (President)	90.36 −2.26 X	−25.6	15.2	20.8
1875–1918 (Governor)	79.23 −2.28 X	−32.6		
1920–1968 (President)	50.20 +1.56 X	+36.2	27.7	13.5
1922–1966 (Governor)	35.29 +2.14 X	+62.9		

since 1914. Moreover, of course, the same institutional differences between these states can be traced back to the 1870's, while the behavioral differences cannot.

Interesting as these findings are, however, and suggestive as they may be of the quite different impacts of the New Deal realignment on a state with a very highly developed socioeconomic system, on the one hand, and a border state with many nineteenth-century survivals, on the other, one major point concerning registration requirements and turnout seems clear. The differences are overwhelmingly systemic, not rules-related. This is obviously the case for the 1876–1916 period, when the rules were largely the same. Even for the contemporary period, it may be worth noting that in 1960 Pennsylvania had statewide personal registration while Missouri had such requirements in an urban-metropolitan minority of its counties which cast 59 per cent of the total statewide vote. Despite this, their turnout rates were virtually identical.[19]

A more detailed examination of turnout within Pennsylvania reveals something of the enormous magnitudes of both the post-1900 decline in the size of the active voting universe and that of the post-1924 increase. Some quantitative estimate of the possible effect of personal registration as an intervening variable can also be made. Prior to 1937, more than half the state's counties, lacking cities of at least the third class within their borders, had no mandatory personal-registration requirements. Indeed, one of the more interesting fruits of the 1935–38 "little New Deal" in Pennsylvania was the complete revamping of the state's election laws, including the extension of personal-registration requirements to all jurisdictions in the state. Because of this convenient division of the state between 1906 and 1937 into registration and nonregistration territory, it becomes possible to construct a straightforward statistical test of both the 1900–16 slump and the 1920–36 recovery (Table 4.4).[20]

The suspicion that far more powerful forces were at work to depress Pennsylvania turnout after 1900 than the introduction of personal registration alone is at once raised by noting that

[19] The Missouri turnout rate in 1960 was 71.8 per cent; in Pennsylvania it was 70.5 per cent.

[20] Unfortunately, not without ambiguity whose complete unraveling would have entailed a prohibitive increment of data compilation. The Pennsylvania statutes covered only cities of the third class and larger. Since only one county—Philadelphia—was coterminous with this coverage, all others which are designated here as "registration territory" in this period had in fact more or less substantial portions of voters who were not covered.

Table 4.4 The Effects of Registration Requirements in
Pennsylvania Turnout, 1900–1936, by
Registration Categories

Year or Period	Mean Turnout Registration Areas	Mean Turnout Nonregistration Areas	t	Significance p
1900	77.8	80.9	1.850	.05 > p > .025
1916	63.0	68.5	3.359	.005 > p > .0005
Mean Shift, 1900–1916	−14.4	−12.4	1.451	.10 > p > .05
1920	41.5	47.1	4.470	p > .0005
1936	66.3	75.7	6.372	p > .0005
Mean Shift, 1920–1936	+24.9	+28.5	2.608	.025 > p > .01

every county in the state shared in this depression. Similarly,
all sixty-seven counties in the state, whether or not they contained registration territory, showed positive slopes on the
1920–36 regression lines. If one applies a standard t test to the
two categories of counties, this evaluation of the difference of
means suggests the plausibility of the hypothesis that registration eventually affected turnout, but there are significant am-
biguities even here.

Employing the more exacting standards of a one-tailed test
—since one can assume in advance that turnout is likely to be
higher where there were no registration requirements than
where such requirements existed—it is clear enough that the
null hypothesis must be rejected for 1916, 1920, and 1936—
that is, for the three points in time after adoption of the 1906
legislation. Assuming a .025 standard for rejection, one can
also presume that registration, or something associated with it
in the same clusters of counties, involved a differential effect
in the 1920–36 upward shift in turnout. But the *downward*

shift along the 1900–16 regression line is a different story. Here it is rather unreasonable to reject the null hypothesis; the difference in the rate of turnout decline between the two groups of counties in this critical period may have been due to some phenomenon having nothing to do with the introduction or effects of personal registration.

The problem becomes more obscure still. Assuming that personal registration was the variable actually measured in Table 4.4—and the evidence is circumstantially very impressive, barring analysis on a level which is still prohibitively minute at this stage—there was a systematic tendency *both before 1906 and after 1937* for Pennsylvania turnout to be correlated inversely with urbanization. The data in selected years is shown in Table 4.5.

Table 4.5 Urbanization and Turnout: Pennsylvania, 1900–1960

Year	Mean Turnout (All Counties)	r (% Turnout, % Urban, Nearest Census)	r^2
1900	79.6	−.398	.159
1916	66.5	−.484	.234
1936	75.5	−.562	.316
1940	66.7	−.370	.137
1960	70.8	−.266	.071

Thus, while it seems evident that factors associated with both urbanization and personal registration were significantly related to differences in turnout, more work than has been done here would be required to disentangle the persistent tendency toward higher turnout in rural areas—all of which were non-registration territory between 1906 and 1937—from differential effects due to registration alone.

What seems to be the most likely explanation of these phenomena is that the introduction of personal registration almost certainly counted for something, and in the direction Kelley's analysis indicates. But putting first things first, one concludes that the systemic forces at work during these periods were far broader in their scope and far heavier in their impact than any single change in the rules of the game or, in all probability, of all such changes put together. Indeed, these forces were the context in which the rules changes occurred, and the subsequent effects of the latter have been heavily influenced by the demands placed on electoral politics at given points in time by those elements of the potential electorate which were then mobilized.[21] They were, in the main, devices by which a large and possibly dangerous mass electorate could be brought to heel and subjected to management and control within the political system appropriate to "capitalist democracy." But they were not the ultimate causes or origins of the conditions which made possible such a remarkable solution to the problem of adjusting mass politics to the exigencies of industrialism.

[21] One notes, for example, that Key's description of the workings of primaries is extremely accurate for Pennsylvania politics from the time of its introduction in 1908 until about 1930. The main contests for power took place within the Republican primary shortly after its introduction, and the usual consequences for the minority party duly appeared. But this ended during the 1930's. Primary participation is apt to be smaller today in absolute numbers than it was during the 1920's, and—unlike the situation in many primary states—the restoration of two-party competition in the New Deal period has involved both the revival and maintenance of minority candidacies in all parts of the state.

5

The Contemporary Scene I:
The Onward March of
Party Decomposition

As the American political system moves into the 1970's, the processes we have described have lost none of their relevance. This proposition might be true in any decade almost by definition, since one of the most remarkable aspects of American politics is its nondevelopmental character. But the significance of both processes, that of realignment and that of disaggregation, seems exceptionally great for the present period because of yet another extraordinary phenomenon. Since at least the mid-1960's increasing evidence has been accumulating that a nationwide critical realignment may be in the making. Yet electoral disaggregation has very obviously undergone immense, almost geometric, expansion in precisely the same period. Since these two processes are inversely related to each other—electoral disaggregation carried beyond a certain point would, after all, make critical realignment in the classical sense impossible—an analytical dilemma arises when one considers the two sets of phenomena together.

It is possible, of course, that this dilemma will be resolved through realignment. That is, the exceptionally rapid erosion of the behavioral hold of the old major parties on the American electorate which is now going on may be part of a pre-realignment process during which masses of voters become available for mobilization along other than traditional lines. Presumably, such realignment would involve the creation of a sixth party system of as yet undefined structure and policy content. Since such a system would be clustered around issues about which many Americans care passionately—at least initially—it would also presumably entail the reinforcement of party-related behavior in the electorate and hence a steep decline in disaggregative phenomena.

Such a pattern would have its own uniqueness. It would not correspond to the realignments of the 1890's, which took place for the most part under conditions of much fuller electoral mobilization than now exists and with very low levels in some indices of disaggregation. Nor would it correspond very closely to the New Deal realignment of the 1930's, since this realignment began from an extremely low base of political participation and rested very largely upon an unevenly distributed ingestion of poor and immigrant-stock whites into the active electorate. Perhaps the closest approximation which could be found would be the realigning decade of the 1850's, which was preceded by both significant declines in participation and by a growing fluidity of the voting support for the old parties, notably the Whigs. It is clear enough in any event that the proportion of the active electorate which is now available for mobilization in some direction other than that which has defined the major contours of the post-1932 party system is already great enough to permit a realignment of enormous magnitude, even by past standards.

When critical realignment is contemplated, it is also necessary to contemplate the nature and magnitude of the stresses arising in society and economy which give some prospect of spilling over into the political arena, and we shall examine this question later. At this point, the observer can report only what he sees: the simultaneous emergence of two trends, each of which is of great practical significance for the workings of the political system, and each of which is inversely related to the other. We shall consider electoral disaggregation in this chapter, critical realignment in the next.

As the preceding chapter has pointed out, the interaction between changes in the rules of the game and substantive changes in voting behavior at the aggregate level—and presumably at the individual level as well—produced both a quantitatively and qualitatively different electorate by 1920 than that which had existed before 1900. The cumulative effect of these rules changes was, with few exceptions, heavily depoliticizing and antipartisan.[1] Moreover, since to this day American politics remains state politics to a very substantial degree, it is worth pointing out that on the state level, rules manipulations and inactions of a distinctly antidemocratic character have persisted to the present.

Three obvious examples of this come to mind. One is an increase in the rotten-borough effects of malapportionment and nonapportionment in state legislatures between the 1930's and

[1] This has been emphasized repeatedly, and accurately by Key, Hays, and others. For a general but extremely provocative account of this transitional era, see Robert H. Wiebe, *The Search for Order, 1877–1920* (New York: Hill & Wang, 1967). It may only be an academician's fancy to see analogies between the development of American electoral politics in this period and the emergence of the English "Venetian Oligarchy" between 1700 and 1720, but a "search for order" which has very similar overtones was going on there during that period, and directed there—as was the post-1896 organization of politics here—against a large and potentially subversive electorate. See J. H. Plumb, *The Growth of Political Stability in England, 1675–1725* (London: Macmillan, 1967).

the mid-1960's. Still another is the growing tendency of states to raise qualifications for third parties to such inordinate heights that none is able to qualify. These two constraints were finally overthrown by a characteristically American "last resort," judicial decision—the first in *Reynolds v. Sims;* the second in 1968.[2] Another practice, which probably cannot be reached by judicial review, is the spreading tendency of states to insulate major state political races from the tides of national electoral politics by scheduling them in off years.[3] To a significant extent this constitutes what may be called legally prescribed electoral disaggregation. Not only does it insure that presidential elections involving the two major parties at their broadest national confrontation will have no immediate effect upon electoral politics in the states, but that electorates of the smallest possible size will determine the outcome of state elections.[4] The scope of this movement may be suggested by Table 5.1.

The origins of movement toward electoral disaggregation are peculiarly associated with the early phase of the fourth elec-

[2] As to the first, the county-unit rule was terminated in *Gray v. Sanders,* 372 U.S. 368 (1963); malapportionment of congressional districts in *Wesberry v. Sanders,* 376 U.S. 1 (1964); and a "one-man-one-vote" apportionment rule for state legislatures was adopted in *Reynolds v. Sims,* 377 U.S. 533 (1964). Finally, the poll-tax requirement for voting in state elections was abolished by the Court in *Harper v. Virginia State Board of Elections,* 383 U.S. 663 (1966). An example of the second was a July 2, 1968, ruling by the Idaho Supreme Court that for the state to prevent George Wallace from organizing and qualifying a third party was a denial of constitutional rights. This was similar to a ruling made shortly afterwards by the U.S. Supreme Court against Ohio. 26 *Congressional Quarterly Weekly Report,* p. 1766 (July 12, 1968).

[3] See V. O. Key, Jr., *American State Politics, op. cit.,* pp. 41–49.

[4] The evidence here is quite persuasive. Dropoff between presidential and off-year elections in the current period involves between one-fifth and one-quarter of the presidential-year electorate. See Walter Dean Burnham, "The Changing Shape of the American Political Universe," 59 *American Political Science Review,* pp. 7–28 (1965); and Angus Campbell, "Surge and Decline: A Study of Electoral Change," in Angus Campbell *et al., Elections and the Political Order, op. cit.,* pp. 40–62.

Table 5.1 Shifting of State Elections from Presidential to Off-Years, 1920–1970

	States Having Major State-Office Elections in:		
Year	Every Presidential Year	One of Three Presidential Years	No Presidential Year
1920	35	1	12
1944	32	1	15
1970	20	–	30

toral system. Returning to Jensen's typology of presidential election campaigns, it is highly suggestive that he finds a major change in the perception of the mass electorate by party leaders and candidates, and an adaptation of their behavior accordingly. This change is first manifested clearly in the 1916 presidential election, and involves a shift from what he calls the "militarist" to the "advertising" (or "mercantilist") campaign style.[5] In view of the considerable body of professional literature which appeared on the subject of election campaigns as exercises in mass-media salesmanship during the 1950's, it is particularly interesting to see that these techniques go back far earlier in time than the Eisenhower era. They were restricted, of course, by the limits of technology and the newness of the enterprise in the second decade of this century: there was as yet no radio, not to mention television, nor was there anything quite analogous to the campaign-management functions which have been assumed in our contemporary electoral politics by outside advertising agencies. But the shift toward this part of the "future of American politics" was evident even then.

The Democrats resorted to these techniques in 1916 for an excellent practical reason: in many of the states Wilson had

[5] Jensen, "American Election Campaigns," *op. cit.*, pp. 18–24.

to carry if he hoped to win re-election, the aftermath of the
1890's had been such that local Democratic organizations were
almost totally ineffective as political mobilizers and communi-
cators. But both parties found the new techniques indispensable for dealing with a very different electorate from those of
the 1880's or 1890's. As Jensen says:

> An appeal must be made to unaffiliated or independent voters,
> and it can no longer be made by reactivation of party loyalty.
> Advertising is the basic technique of the mercantilistic style,
> and the voters are treated like potential consumers of mer-
> chandise. . . . Each candidate on a ticket is free to package
> his own appeal, more or less independently of his running
> mates. . . . Candidates appeal primarily to undecided and
> wavering voters of both parties—last-minute shoppers, as it
> were—and often ignore their party's traditional image in mak-
> ing a sustained sales pitch to potential customers in the com-
> petitor's market area.[6]

The emergence of the advertising type of political campaign
was conditioned by the new circumstances of politics created
during the early part of the fourth electoral era. Candidates
and party managers perceived that a new structure of mass
behavior was coming into existence, and they perceived cor-
rectly. As the "militarist" political style was perfectly suited
to a political world of fully mobilized electorates, multiple but
enduring party formations, close competition, and convention
nominations, so the "mercantilist" style was adapted to a political world of shrunken electorates, direct primaries, and steep
declines in public response to partisanship even among those
who remained in the active electorate. As it would have been
futile to attempt to win most pre-1896 elections by converting
a largely nonexistent "floating vote," so it became increasingly
pointless for parties to engage either in activities designed to
produce the highest possible turnout of their supporters—who

[6] *Ibid.*, pp. 18–19.

were supporters by 1916 or 1920?—or in such activities as
selective but effective bribery of voters.[7] Bribery makes sense
only under conditions of fairly perfect information; the less
perfect the information, the greater the escalation in cost, until
the point of diminishing returns or bankruptcy is achieved.

The shift to an advertising-oriented set of campaign styles
and strategies was an effect rather than a cause of the grass-
roots changes which also produced modern electoral disaggregation, but it in turn contributed to its further development.
Not only does such a campaign style correspond to a regime
marked by the kind of dissolution of party we have outlined,
it also contributes to it. Of course, such contribution in its turn
does not *determine* that parties will evaporate and cease to
perform meaningful linkage functions for the electorate, even
in the choice of candidates: when major issues of interest
aggregation and reallocation of scarce resources arise with
sufficient intensity, as they did during the 1930's, the influence
of party will tend to increase, even during the present era. It
will nevertheless, *ceteris paribus,* contribute to that long-run
result.

Not only is the evidence very clear that the origins of electoral disaggregation are to be found in the turn-of-the-century
reorganization of politics, it is equally clear that the development of this phenomenon has resumed with redoubled force
since the early 1950's, after an interval of decline during the
height of the New Deal realignment.

Turning first to the New Deal realignment, we note that it
differed in certain significant respects from its predecessors.

---

[7] This, of course, is not to say that such practices *disappeared,* particularly in machine-controlled cities where they not infrequently lasted until
and even beyond the New Deal. But for a variety of reasons associated
both with the policy implications of solid Republicanism in the North
and solid Democratic loyalty in the South after 1896, and with the
carrying out of progressive-era reforms, their locus tended to shift downward in the political system.

Of course, there had been numerous harbingers of realignment in the nineteenth century, in some cases appearing years before the critical-election convulsion took place. But these earlier critical realignments themselves had two quite impressive characteristics: they occurred with extreme rapidity once the process of realignment actually got underway, and they tended to affect electoral politics at all levels within the system more or less simultaneously. For instance, the Kansas-Nebraska Act became law on May 30, 1854. The initial, decisive stage of the Civil War realignment in a Yankee community such as St. Lawrence County, New York, can be pinpointed as falling between the elections of November 1853 and November 1854. The electorates of probably hundreds of counties scattered throughout the New England diaspora behaved similarly at about that time. So too with the realignment of the 1890's. Using a number of state elections as benchmarks, it is fair to say that the flash point of critical realignment was reached at some point between April and November of 1893—that is, almost instantaneously with the onset of the great financial panic and depression of that year. It is also significant that Democratic candidates in Ohio and Iowa in the fall 1893 elections tried to dissociate themselves from national issues, and that, if the judgment of contemporary observers may be credited, they failed. National issues had a major impact on these campaigns, and the Democratic in Party in Ohio, for example, suffered the worst electoral defeat since the anti-Vallandigham landslide of 1863.[8]

When one compares the realignment patterns of the 1850's and 1890's with the critical elections associated with the 1929 Depression and the New Deal, the latter suggest a far muddier pattern of electoral readjustment than the former. There is an impression of "crispness," of a clean break, in the earlier data

[8] *Appleton's Annual Cyclopedia . . . of the Year 1893* (New York: D. Appleton, 1894), pp. 409–10, 590–91.

which is not apparent in the 1930's when one takes state as well
as presidential elections into account. As we have seen, for
example, the Pennsylvania data indicate that in some respects
the 1924 Progressive vote and the 1928 election were parts of
a process of critical realignment, but—in terms of aggregate
behavior, at least—it is much more difficult to make this judgment about the election of 1932, either locally or nationally.

Even at that, critical realignment in Pennsylvania, while it
was a far longer and more complex process in the 1930's than
in the 1890's, led to clean-cut results by comparison with many
other parts of the country. One whole region of the country—
the South—underwent almost no realignment for decades after
1932, with the most obvious consequences for executive-con-
gressional cooperation in policy-making after 1938. While Dixie
tended to "rejoin the union" at the presidential level in and
after 1952, not until a series of judicial decisions and acts of
Congress were handed down in the mid-1960's were the region's oligarchic electorate-control devices seriously undermined, and the conditions created for the disintegration of the
region's traditional Democratic hegemony.

But unevenness of realignment effects during the New Deal
era was by no means confined to southern deviations from a
national pattern. The growing divergence of coalitional patterns in state and presidential elections has been documented
for the state of Ohio.[9] Moreover, throughout a number of
western and northwestern states there was very limited con-
gruence of voting behavior between presidential contests and
state or congressional elections for many years after 1932.

This was most obviously the case in states like Wisconsin and
Minnesota, in which leftist local parties cornered most of the
opposition to the Republicans at the state level until the end

[9] Thomas A. Flinn, "Continuity and Change in Ohio Politics," 24 *Journal of Politics*, pp. 521–44 (1964); and John H. Fenton, *Midwest Politics, op. cit.*, pp. 117–54.

of World War II. It is scarcely less obvious in the case of
North Dakota, where bifactional rivalry within Republican
primaries was the usual alternative to interparty competition
between about 1916 and 1958. In other states concentrated in
the great northwestern and western arc of La Follette's 1924
strength—states with semicolonial traditions which had been
thoroughly developed since the turn of the century—one need
merely look beneath the surface of formal two-party competition to find striking discrepancies between behavior on the
presidential level and in state elections, not to mention discrepancies, particularly before about 1945, between both Democrats and Republicans elected in these local electoral sub-
systems and the national party leadership of the time.

One extremely suggestive range of quantitatively measurable
change which bears upon this proposition is found in the
phenomenon that Nelson Polsby has called "the institutionalization of the House of Representatives." [10] Although this
process is not directly associated with mass electoral behavior
as such, it correlates temporally—as we shall see—with
changes in that behavior as it relates to congressional elections.

Polsby has provided us with data for the period from the
47th through the 88th Congresses (1881–1963) which yields
the percentage of times in which seniority was followed in
committee chairmanship assignments (see Table 5.2).[11] The
evaluative procedure used is essentially identical with that
discussed earlier for establishing cutting points for realignment. As before, a t test of discrepancy between means has
been derived longitudinally for each contiguous set of ten Congresses. The result is as dramatic as it is unambiguous. During
this period, t reaches two and only two maxima: at midpoint

[10] Nelson W. Polsby, "The Institutionalization of the House of Representatives," 62 *American Politcial Science Review*, pp. 144–68 (1968).
[11] Nelson W. Polsby *et al.*, "The Growth of the Seniority System in
the House of Representatives," 63 *American Political Science Review*,
pp. 787–807 (1969), at p. 792.

Table 5.2 Trends and Cutting-Points in Congressional Rules: The Growth of the Seniority Norm, 1881–1969

Congresses	Midpoint Year	% Seniority, House Committee Chairmanships		
		M_1	M_2	t
47th–56th	1890	34.0	48.9	1.080
48th–57th	1892	38.1	61.0	1.856
49th–58th	1894	44.1	66.7	1.904
50th–59th	1896	38.6	79.0	6.166
51st–60th	1898	42.7	80.7	4.387
52nd–61st	1900	48.9	79.9	2.874
53rd–62nd	1902	61.0	72.3	0.909
54th–63rd	1904	66.7	68.9	0.173
55th–64th	1906	79.0	69.5	1.231
56th–65th	1908	80.7	70.3	1.354
57th–66th	1910	79.9	68.6	1.408
58th–67th	1912	72.3	73.9	0.180
59th–68th	1914	68.9	75.5	0.811
60th–69th	1916	69.5	70.1	0.086
61st–70th	1918	70.3	73.3	0.309
62nd–71st	1920	68.6	77.9	0.971
63rd–72nd	1922	73.9	75.0	0.125
64th–73rd	1924	75.5	77.8	0.276
65th–74th	1926	70.1	79.5	1.255
66th–75th	1928	73.3	78.2	0.570
67th–76th	1930	77.9	77.4	0.059
68th–77th	1932	75.0	82.4	0.946
69th–78th	1934	77.8	80.6	0.351
70th–79th	1936	79.5	82.5	0.428
71st–80th	1938	78.2	78.1	0.026
72nd–81st	1940	77.4	82.0	0.606
73rd–82nd	1942	82.4	85.0	0.368
74th–83rd	1944	80.6	88.8	1.163
75th–84th	1946	82.5	92.7	1.564
76th–85th	1948	78.1	98.9	7.219

Table 5.2 Trends and Cutting-Points in Congressional
Rules: The Growth of the Seniority Norm, 1881–1969 (*Cont.*)

Congresses	Midpoint Year	*% Seniority, House Committee Chairmanships*		
		M_1	M_2	*t*
77th–86th	1950	82.0	98.9	3.178
78th–87th	1952	85.0	98.9	2.143
79th–88th	1954	88.8	100.0	1.845
80th–89th	1956	92.7	99.0	1.036
81st –90th	1958	98.9	99.0	0.080
82nd–91st	1960	98.9	99.0	0.080

1896 (the set covering the 50th–59th Congresses) it leaps up
to 6.166, and at midpoint 1948 (the set covering the 76th–85th
Congresses), it shows a sudden increase to 7.219. With the
exception of the two t scores following each of these upheavals,
no other in the entire array of thirty-six sets is as large as 2.

Clearly, the second t upheaval is intimately associated with
the changes in congressional rules associated with the
Legislative Reorganization Act of 1946. This act, whose
purpose was believed by some to be the modernization of
congressional procedures and structures, greatly increased the
scarcity of a supremely valuable resource, the chairmanship of
committees. It seems to be the most likely causal agency by
which the mean percentage of seniority selection of chairmen
increased from 78.1 per cent for the 76th through the 80th
Congresses (1939–47) to 98.9 per cent for the 81st through the
85th (1949–57). In a quite typically American fashion, "modernization" thus seems to have entailed a further movement
toward "institutionalization." In this case, the movement was
toward an approximation of the maximum possible fragmentation of the House's leadership structure: the processes of

seniority, by their very automatic character, operate virtually independently of any wishes which a central party leadership, whether in the House or elsewhere, might have on the matter.

The earlier peak in t represents not the effect of a rules change but a behavioral change, although it is in the norms by which an elective elite chooses its internal leadership rather than in mass behavior. It goes without saying that the midpoint year of peak behavioral transition, 1896, falls in the middle of the transition between the third and fourth party systems in the mass electorate. Here, as in so many other aspects of change in this political system, the transformation was essentially toward the modern shape of American politics. The timing of this change is neither coincidental nor accidental. Before the mid-1890s, there was very large fluctuation in the proportion of committee chairmanships selected on seniority grounds; the norm had simply not been fully institutionalized. Afterward, a high and relatively stable reliance on seniority came quite abruptly into being. It would be surprising indeed if the sudden upward shift in this reliance on seniority were not somehow related to the essentially negative public-policy purposes of the new majority coalition.

These findings are of particular interest in two respects. First, it is clear that the transition to a stable norm of primary reliance on seniority in the choice of committee chairmen cannot be traced to the time when Speaker Cannon's powers were stripped in 1910, but nearly half a generation earlier. In fact, the overthrow of Cannon may well have been effect rather than cause: his pretensions to control—perhaps arising from the inflexibility of a man whose service in the House began at a time when a very different set of norms prevailed—were incompatible with a norm which had come solidly into being before his own election to the Speakership. The transition into a thoroughly "modern" structure of House institutionalization was a long-drawn-out process probably not achieved until about 1920, but the emergence of a stable norm of seniority in the middle 1890's clearly inaugurated the process.

Second, the data leave no doubt that the New Deal realignment, however massive at the grass roots and however significant in reorganizing the scope and focus of national policy, left the behavioral routines of the House almost completely untouched, at least as far as seniority was concerned. If it is important in evaluating any change to describe what did *not* happen as a result as well as what did, the failure of a new congressional policy structure to emerge after the 1928–36 realignment seems particularly instructive. It pinpoints one set of limiting conditions—a context which eventually circumscribed severely the New Deal's innovative capacities. The post-New Deal transition, which appears to be largely an artifact of a supposedly modernizing rules change, has now virtually completed the linear process of disaggregation in policy structures inaugurated during the 1890's.

One other aspect of institutionalization which closely follows this pattern is what might be described as the "professionalization of the Speaker." A century and more ago half or more of the members of the House at any given time were likely to be freshmen. Similarly, before the 1890's the tenure of Speakers in the House prior to their election tended to be much shorter than is the case today. To take two extreme cases: when William Pennington was elected Speaker as a compromise candidate in 1860, he was a freshman; when John McCormack was elected speaker in 1962, he was in his thirty-fourth consecutive year in the House.

If one evaluates changes in the mean tenure of Speakers at the time of their first election to the Speakership over the 1834–1962 period, a pattern closely similar to that found for the growth of the seniority norm—and for mass presidential-year turnout, for that matter—is found (see Table 5.3 and Chart 5.1). There is only one peak in t for the series of twenty-four contiguous ten-election sets of Speakership elections. It

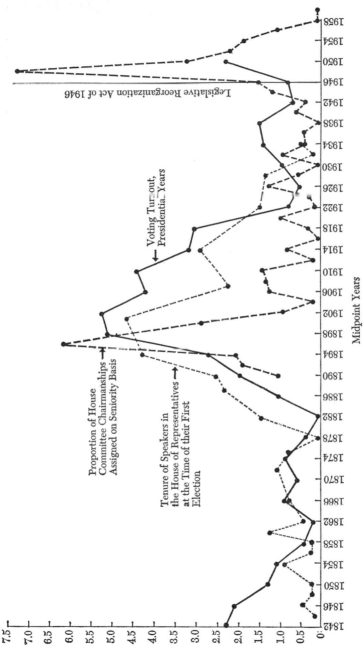

Chart 5.1 Turn-of-the-Century Transformations in the American Political System: Three Indicators

falls midway between the first elections of Charles Crisp (Democrat, 1891) and David Henderson (Republican, 1899), with t = 4.243; and midway between the first election of Henderson in 1899 and of Joseph G. Cannon (Republican, 1903), with t = 4.673.[12] A simpler way of making this point, perhaps, is to note that the mean tenure of the five Speakers from J. Warren Keifer (Republican, 1881) to Henderson was 9.4 years at the time of their first election, while the mean tenure of the five Speakers from Cannon in 1903 to John N. Garner in 1931 had risen to twenty-four years at the time of their first election. Here, as has been noted earlier, the electoral realignment of the 1890's was closely associated chronologically with basic institutional change; the change was unidirectional rather than periodical or cyclical; and the subsequent realignment of the 1930's was not associated with any significant change in the pattern which had thus been established.

Nor is disaggregation associated with the House of Representatives confined only to its internal structure of rules and norms. Milton Cummings has recently demonstrated the modern growth of divergent outcomes in concurrent presidential and congressional elections at the congressional-district level.[13] One primary aspect of electoral disaggregation, of course, is the "pulling apart" over time of vote percentages for the same party but at different levels of election. To pursue the long-term trends in concurrent presidential-congressional elections, we have somewhat extended and rearranged two of Cummings' tables. His argument seems obviously confirmed: the gross effects of split-ticket voting, already quite massive during the 1920's, were considerably constricted during the height of the New Deal period but have subsequently under-

---

[12] In other words, at midpoint years 1894/95 and 1901, respectively.
[13] Milton Cummings, *Congressmen and the Electorate* (Glencoe, Ill.: The Free Press, 1967).

Table 5.3 Trends and Cutting-Points in Congressional Norms: Tenure of Speakers at First Election to Speakership, 1834–1962

Speakers	Number	Midpoint Year	Mean Tenure at First Election (Years) M₁	M₂	t
Bell (W)–Banks (R)	1–10	1844	6.6	7.0	0.176
Polk (D)–Orr (D)	2–11	1846	6.4	7.4	0.442
Hunter (D)– Pennington (R)	3–12	1848	5.6	6.2	0.234
White (W)–Grow (R)	4–13	1850	6.4	7.0	0.238
Jones (D)–Colfax (R)	5–14	1854	8.0	5.8	0.910
Davis (D)–Blaine (R)	6–15	1856	7.0	6.4	0.238
Winthrop (W)–Kerr (D)	7–16	1858	7.4	6.8	0.230
Cobb (D)–Randall (D)	8–17	1860	6.2	9.4	1.209
Boyd (D)–Keifer (R)	9–18	1862	7.0	8.2	0.408
Banks (R)–Carlisle (D)	10–19	1866	5.8	7.8	0.811
Orr (D)–Reed (R)	11–20	1872	6.4	9.0	1.065
Pennington (R)– Crisp (D)	12–21	1875	6.8	8.8	0.792
Grow (R)– Henderson (R)	13–22	1878	9.4	9.4	0.000
Colfax (R)–Cannon (R)	14–23	1882	8.2	14.2	1.452
Blaine (R)–Clark (D)	15–24	1887	7.8	16.2	2.323
Kerr (D)–Gillett (R)	16–25	1890	9.0	19.0	2.548
Randall (D)– Longworth (R)	17–26	1894	8.8	21.6	4.243
Keifer (R)–Garner (D)	18–27	1901	9.4	24.0	4.673
Carlisle (D)– Rainey (D)	19–28	1907	14.2	24.0	2.200
Reed (D)–Byrns (D)	20–29	1914	16.2	26.0	2.872
Crisp (D)– Bankhead (D)	21–30	1922	19.0	24.6	1.420
Henderson (R)– Rayburn (D)	22–31	1928	21.6	25.6	1.332
Cannon (R)–Martin (R)	23–32	1932	24.0	24.4	0.141
Clark (D)– McCormack (D)	24–33	1934	24.0	25.4	0.425

gone renewed increases. One may begin with a simple measure which Cummings employed, the proportion of split outcomes at the congressional-district level. In Table 5.4 the series has been pushed back to 1900 and ahead to 1968.[14] It seems evident not only that the series has a rather steep upward trend [15] but that the increase toward roughly "modern" levels must be pushed back at least to 1916. Split results in the nineteenth century, one may assume, were on the whole at least as infrequent as in the first two elections of this series.

If one turns to the examination of the popular-vote spread by district between 1920 and 1968, one notes an analogous and very marked movement toward greater and greater spread in the outcomes of the two elections. Rearranging Cummings' data and extending it to 1968, we have the pattern shown in Table 5.5.[16]

Taking the two tables together, a clear pattern of electoral disaggregation emerges. At first almost nonexistent, it rises steeply during the second decade of this century and peaks temporarily in the 1920's. It then falls rapidly (but probably only to the levels of the 1910–20 period rather than to earlier ones) during the New Deal era, but once again resumes upward movement in the 1950's and reaches record highs during

[14] This is a composite of Tables 2.1 (p. 32) and 5.1 (p. 139) in Cummings, *op. cit.*, with continuation of the data series for 1900–16 and 1968.

[15] $Y_c = 2.28 + 1.50\,X$. Regressing on time gives a coefficient of $+.809$ and a squared coefficient of $.654$.

[16] Adapted from Cummings, *op. cit.*, Table 2.2 (p. 37). The regression lines and coefficients for the 1920–68 period, and for each column, are:

Spread	$Y_c =$	r (time)	r^2 (time)
0–2.4%	$42.92 - 1.84\,X$	$-.610$	.372
2.5–4.9%	$18.29 - 0.00\,X$	$-.005$	.000
5–9.9%	$16.85 + 0.41\,X$	$+.417$	.165
10% and Over	$15.17 + 3.89\,X$	$+.578$	.335
0–4.9%	$61.20 - 1.84\,X$	$-.565$	.320
5% and Over	$38.80 + 1.84\,X$	$+.565$	.320

Table 5.4 Proportion of Split Results: Congress and President, 1900–1968

Year	Number of Districts Analyzed	% of Split Results	% of Splits Involving Minor Party
1900	295	3.4	0
1904	310	1.6	0
1908	314	6.8	0
1912	333	25.2	50.0
1916	333	10.3	0
1920	344	3.2	0
1924	356	11.8	28.6
1928	359	18.9	1.5
1932	355	14.1	10.0
1936	361	14.1	19.6
1940	362	14.6	9.4
1944	367	11.2	2.4
1948	422	22.5	33.7
1952	435	19.3	1.2
1956	435	29.9	1.5
1960	437	26.1	2.6
1964	435	33.3	0
1968	435	31.7	34.8

the 1960's. Without attempting to derive formulas which would give more precise estimates, we can summarize these movements thus: if the close pre-1900 partisan integration of voting behavior at all levels had continued to exist to the present time, in 1956 the Republicans would have won nearly 300 seats instead of the 200 they actually secured, and in 1964 the Democrats would have elected between 330 and 350 congressmen, instead of the 295 actually elected.

We have already suggested certain behavioral realities in our analysis of electoral change in Pennsylvania during the

Table 5.5 Electoral Disaggregation: Increases in
Dispersion of Major-Party Percentages for President and
Congress by Congressional District, 1920–1968

*Spread Between Percentage Democratic of Two-Party Vote
for President and Congress*

Year	0–2.4%	2.5–4.9%	5–9.9%	10 % and Over	Under 5%	5% and Over
1920	47.3	14.7	14.2	23.8	62.0	38.0
1924	19.9	19.1	25.0	36.0	39.0	61.0
1928	24.2	15.4	20.6	39.8	39.6	60.4
1932	47.6	18.6	17.7	16.1	66.2	33.8
1936	41.3	24.1	18.0	16.6	65.4	34.6
1940	38.4	19.9	14.9	26.8	58.3	41.7
1944	35.7	21.2	18.0	25.1	56.9	43.1
1948	34.1	15.0	18.9	32.0	49.1	50.9
1952	32.0	20.0	15.4	32.6	52.0	48.0
1956	16.0	16.0	25.1	42.3	32.0	68.0
1960	22.0	18.7	22.2	37.1	40.7	59.3
1964	18.6	17.5	20.5	43.4	36.1	63.9
1968	13.8	17.2	25.8	43.2	31.0	69.0

1850's which may shed light on the political strategy followed
by the Radical Republicans in the late 1860's. Similarly, a
review of the extent to which realignment in the 1930's was
not accompanied or followed by changes in electoral behavior
(as in the South) or by changes in key policy structures (as in
the House of Representatives) provides us with some clues
for evaluating elite political strategies during the latter period.

For example, it is hardly surprising that Roosevelt's response
to this diffuse, rather incoherent context should have included
his attempted 1938 "purge" of anti-New Deal Democrats in
Congress or that he should have lost that campaign. It is also
understandable that the committed New Dealers in his administration attempted from time to time to raise the standard of

a new "progressive" party which would at last give them the leverage they needed to carry out their policy objectives—and this at almost precisely the time when the New Deal realignment at the mass base was reaching its consummation.[17] For, in truth, the Democratic Party and electoral politics in general had become very blunt instruments for governing or for generating the power links needed to coordinate the presidency and Congress as component parts of the national policy-making process. The disaggregation of both electoral behavior and policy which had been unleashed during the fourth party system survived that system's demise in many key areas of our political life. It may be argued, in fact, that the New Deal realignment did not terminate or even reverse that dispersion of the potential resources of the public sector; instead, it revealed to all that it had become institutionalized—probably permanently—in our political system.

It is possible to evaluate the increasing "pulling apart" of voting behavior across time in yet another way, by examining voting behavior for the 1880–1968 period within a number of selected states. (See Appendix tables.) What we have done here is to take analytical advantage of that reformer's bugbear, the long ballot. Partisan percentages for each office where the state at large is the constituency have been computed. From these means, variances and standard deviations have been derived, and measures of turnout, dropoff, and rolloff (or net percentage of incompete ballots) have been included.[18] The variances and standard deviations provide a straightforward descriptive measure of net changes in split-ticket voting over time. The higher they are, the closer they

---

[17] See, for example, *The Secret Diary of Harold L. Ickes*, Vol. II (New York: Simon & Schuster, 1954), especially pp. 393–95, 460–74, 696–700.
[18] The dropoff and rolloff measures are discussed and defined in Walter Dean Burnham, "The Changing Shape of the American Political Universe, *op. cit.*

come to Jensen's model "mercantilist" campaign style, in which
each candidate packages and sells himself to a volatile electorate.

One of the five states selected for analysis—Indiana—may
be regarded as a limiting case. This state has probably retained more of both the legal-structural and behavioral attributes of nineteenth-century electoral politics than any other.
It has a very long partisan ballot, with facilities for making
straight-ticket voting as easy as possible. It has retained a well-
known system of state nominating conventions and continues
to fuel the engines of political war with a large-scale patronage
apparatus. Finally, as Table 1 in the Appendix reveals, it has
remained on the whole closely competitive politically from
the 1890's to the present. As one might expect, a comparison of
the state tables in the Appendix reveals that Indiana shows
incomparably more evidence of tightly integrated and party-
oriented voting behavior than any of the other states. In only
nine out of forty-five elections do the mean percentages Democratic exceed 55 or fall below 45; and never do they exceed
60 or fall below 40. Similarly, there is almost no linear partisan
trend up or down over this long period. The variances and
standard deviations are also extremely low throughout, indicative of the failure of split-ticket voting to develop in the
state on any large scale. Finally, turnout rates remain relatively
high, while dropoff between presidential and off-year elections
is low, conditions which were maintained even during the national trough of the 1920's.

The reasons for the perpetuation of these political conditions
in Indiana have been explored by others and need no detailed
discussion here.[19] It is enough to restate what observers of
Indiana politics have pointed out. In no sense can this remarkable example of partisan discipline at the polls be re-

[19] Cf. Fenton, *Midwest Politics, op. cit.,* pp. 155–93.

garded as evidence of evolution toward a twentieth-century model of "responsible parties" which are programmatic and polarized around issues relevant to the central questions of power in an industrial society. The closest approximation to such parties to be found in recent American political history is probably the partisan system in Michigan. Yet Samuel Eldersveld's penetrating analysis of Michigan parties at the height of the "responsible" period—about 1956—demonstrates just how limited such "responsibility" was even at its most focal point,[20] and political disaggregation in that state during the 1960's has turned out to be quite as massive as it has been elsewhere. As far as Indiana politics is concerned, it is quint-essentially "individualist" in political culture and style, to borrow Daniel Elazar's typology, and strongly oriented toward jobs and away from "issues" of any transcendental sort.[21] This remarkably cohesive partisan system thus reflects not political *development* toward new organizational form and behavioral patterns, but a remarkably durable *survival* from the nineteenth-century political universe.

It is to the other four states—Massachusetts, Michigan, Rhode Island, and Wisconsin—that one might more appropriately turn for evidence of sequential development of coherent new structures of collective action. What is found instead is a cumulative, if interrupted and not wholly uniform, pattern of emergent incoherence. Let us begin by discussing the contexts of behavioral change in these states.

Each of these states adopted the Australian ballot between 1889 and 1891. Massachusetts, a pioneer in this reform, organized its ballot in the office-block format which it has kept ever since. The other three followed variants of the party-

[20] Samuel J. Eldersveld, *Political Parties: A Behavioral Analysis* (Chicago: Rand McNally, 1964), especially pp. 440–91, 524–44.
[21] Daniel J. Elazar, *American Federalism: A View from the States* (New York: T. Y. Crowell, 1966), pp. 85–103.

column format. Except for Rhode Island, all these states adopted the direct primary during the height of the movement toward direct democracy: Wisconsin, leading the parade, in 1903; Michigan in 1909; and Massachusetts in 1911. While Rhode Island adopted a primary law in the 1950's, this vehicle of popular government has remained strictly secondary to party organization decisions in the determination of nominations. Finally, all four of these states were heavily affected, though in somewhat differing degrees, by the realignments of the 1890's and 1930's. In all of them, the Democratic Party had reached virtually full parity with the Republicans by the early 1890's, only to be thrust into a virtually hopeless minority position after 1894 in Michigan and Wisconsin and into a somewhat less than hopeless position in Massachusetts and Rhode Island. Similarly, solid Republican one-partyism was abruptly terminated after 1930 in the two states of the upper Midwest, and a modified Republican one-partyism in the two New England states came to an end as a consequence of the 1928 mobilization and its aftermath.

Turning first to an obvious rules-of-the-game change, the introduction of the Australian ballot, it can be seen by inspection of Tables 1–5 in the Appendix that no immediate behavioral change occurred at all except in the percentage of incomplete ballots cast, or "rolloff." [22]

[22] Application of a t test for differences between two means—each derived from a series of five elections before and after the introduction of the change—reveals what is actually a somewhat more mixed pattern than is implied here. Rolloff differentials are extremely marked in Massachusetts, Rhode Island, and Indiana (4.378, 3.157, and 3.508 respectively), but much less so in Michigan (1.697) and very little in Wisconsin (0.570). There is likewise a heavy differential revealed in the percentage Democratic for Michigan (3.250) and Indiana (4.646), and a fairly substantial one in Wisconsin (1.998). This, however, is obviously due to the temporal coincidence within our ten-election framework of the introduction of the Australian ballot and the onset of critical realignment in the 1890's. Were this controlled, the statement in the text would need no amendment.

Here the transition for party-prepared "tickets" to state-printed ballots led to immediate marginal consequences which were most notable in Massachusetts—as could be expected, in view of its adoption of the office-block ballot form. Then, beginning in 1894, the Democratic partisan percentages were severely depressed. While there were isolated instances in all these states of some increases in variance between 1880 and 1900, the norm remained overwhelmingly that of straight-ticket voting. This was true even in Massachusetts, where to cast a straight ballot after 1889 required exceptional attentiveness on the voter's part.

The point at which a considerable increase in variance with a residual long-term increase occurred can be identified for these states quite closely. Rhode Island begins the sequence in 1902. All four states show massive increases in these partisan variances in the 1904 election, and all but Rhode Island show an ascending curve through the 1920's. These behavioral changes, changes away from party as the single predominant guide to voter decision at the polls, seem to be rather directly related to profound changes in the political culture at which our measures merely hint. But they are in no immediate way the effects of changes in such rules as those governing ballot forms—or, as far as one can tell from extremely fragmentary evidence, the introduction of personal-registration requirements.

During and after the 1920's, our states diverge. While turnout declined to some extent after the enfranchisement of women in the two New England states, the minimum in Massachusetts was 46.1 per cent in 1922 and in Rhode Island 52.2 per cent in the same year—both quite respectable turnout figures for off-year elections even in the current era. Nor was there much evidence of growth in electoral "slack" over time.[23]

---

[23] "Slack" here refers to increases in dropoff from presidential to off years as the overall size of the voting universe contracted.

Clearly, this is linked to local political conditions: in these two states, the most industrialized in the country and among the most ethnically heterogeneous, the Democratic Party was never as far away from electoral success during the fourth electoral era—and especially during the 1920's—as presidential-election percentages alone would suggest. On the whole, it would be stretching a point to call the electoral politics of either state fully competitive until 1928, but it was far more so there in the Era of Normalcy than in Michigan or Wisconsin.

In the two midwestern states, by contrast, the development of politics after the 1890's more closely approximated Pennsylvania than Massachusetts. Declines in turnout, increases in electoral slack, the virtual disappearance of the Democratic Party, and steep increases in variances were all intimately related in time. In Wisconsin, the 1904 increase in variance was not resumed until 1912, but then it took off with a vengeance, peaking under nominally "two-party" conditions in the 1920's and at an even higher level during the three-party interlude of 1934–42. The proportion of incomplete ballots crested during the 1920–30 period also, and the decline in turnout brought participation down as low as 34.2 per cent (1922). In Michigan the pattern was very similar, although without the transitional third-party phenomenon found in Wisconsin during the 1934–42 period. Variances took off in 1904 as turnout underwent secular decline, and dropoff gradually increased thereafter.

In all these states the New Deal realignment—first in the New England states, where it was fused into the "Al Smith Revolution" of 1928, and last in Wisconsin—brought about the reversal of these trends toward electoral disaggregation. One is tempted to speculate that as basic political issues come to the center of the electoral stage and party is revitalized as an instrument of constituent politics, the significance of individual candidates and of candidate charisma declines except at the very highest levels.[24] It is clear in any event that from the late 1920's until sometime in the 1950's the structure of electoral politics tended toward a much tighter integration than had been the case earlier in the century. Again, but in reverse, one can perceive the same interactive pattern: increases in party competition and turnout, declines in variance and in electoral slack. The most spectacular example of this is Rhode Island, a state with exceptionally influential party organizations and intense class-ethnic antagonisms which fit well into the classic New Deal-era coalitional pattern.[25] Of the fourteen elections held there between 1928 and 1954, only three showed variances in excess of 1.

It is in this context that the most recent electoral trends in these states become of exceptional interest. To be sure, there has been only the smallest secular trend toward decline in voter participation since 1952, and only in Wisconsin can a faint trend toward increase in dropoff be detected. The variances, however, are an entirely different matter. Beginning with 1956, all these states show disaggregative trends which are little short of geometric progressions. In 1968 variance hit the highest point in Wisconsin since 1928, excluding the special conditions of 1934–40. The figures for 1964 and 1966 for the other three states are the highest—in Massachusetts and Rhode Island, incomparably the highest—in the entire eighty-five-year period under review.[26] While the 1964 result may be dismissed as simply an artifact of the unique conditions surrounding the Goldwater debacle, the extremely high figures for 1966 and 1968 cannot. Moreover, there is no good reason why 1964 should be so dismissed. In the first place, earlier

[24] Even here such visible leadership charisma may be "issue-oriented charisma." See V. O. Key, Jr., *The Responsible Electorate* (Cambridge: Harvard University Press, 1966), pp. 29–62.

[25] See Lockard, *op. cit.*, pp. 172–227.

[26] It might be useful to put these exceptional contemporary variances in more "visible" form. The 1966 Massachusetts variance of 139.03 (standard deviation of 11.79) corresponds to the following percentages Demo-

presidential landslides—whether those of 1904, 1920, 1936, or even 1956—produced no such extreme results; and second, there are many grounds other than those discussed here for assuming that the sequence of elections beginning in 1964 corresponds to a "time of troubles" for the United States fully equal to any of its predecessors, if quite different in some of its measurable properties.

The 1964 election, in fact, seemed at first blush to have many of the characteristics of a realigning election. Indeed, it may come to be widely regarded as the beginning of a realignment sequence. It was an election dominated both by a highly abnormal nomination process in the Republican Party and by massive, unusually issue-oriented movements of large minorities of voters from their traditional partisan moorings in presidential elections. Most significantly, in the light of subsequent developments, in certain ways it bore more resemblance to elections held during the 1896–1932 period than to any since.[27]

Nevertheless, in another important respect the 1964 election was decisively different from any previous election in a

---

cratic of the two-party vote for all offices where the state at large was the electoral constituency:

U.S. Senator	39.0
Governor	37.1
Lieutenant Governor	44.8
Attorney General	47.7
Secretary of the Commonwealth	70.7
Treasurer	63.5
Auditor	57.7

Such an array represents an extreme, but not entirely unique, case in which each candidate must package and market his own campaign, since party identification in the electorate obviously counts for very little in general-election results. It corresponds closely to the marked fragmentation of Massachusetts politics which has been described by V. O. Key, Jr., Edgar Litt, and Murray B. Levin.

[27] Walter Dean Burnham, "American Voting Behavior and the 1964 Election," *op. cit.*

critical-alignment sequence. The steep rise in split-ticket voting in this election was associated with an exceptionally widespread voter solicitude for the political fortunes of Republican candidates who deviated from the rightist campaign being waged at the top of their party's ticket. Such a structure of electoral results suggests that even under conditions of exceptional issue-polarization focused at the presidential level, a very large fraction of the American electorate was unwilling or unable to think of this polarization in *partisan* terms.

This kind of voter discrimination among individual candidates may be regarded by some as desirable. Others may prefer to see candidates of a national political party suffer the conesquences of a decision by the party's top leadership to force a polarization of the electorate on grounds of its own choosing, whatever the divergent policy views of such candidates may be. Whatever one's personal preferences, the empirical evidence supports the growing systemic importance of this differentiation at the polls. It is difficult to square such a development with any model of political behavior in which party plays a decisive role in aggregate voting decisions; it grows more difficult, of course, as the scope of this development continues to widen over time.

A longitudinal analysis of survey results over the past two decades, even at the grossest level, also shows an accelerating trend toward erosion of party linkages in the American electorate, and at two levels: that of voting behavior and that of a normally much more glacial measure, party identification. Since 1948 the Survey Research Center of the University of Michigan has asked its respondents whether they voted straight or split tickets for state and local officials, and since 1952 they have been asked whether they voted for the same party's candidates for president in all elections for which they were eligible, or for candidates of different parties. In Table 5.6

these two series show a sharp break downward during the 1960's.[28]

Table 5.6 The Decline of Party: Evidences from Survey Data, 1948–1966 *

Category	1948	1952	1956	1958	1960	1962	1964	1966
Straight ticket, state and local	72	74	71	70	73	58	60	50
Same party's presidential candidate	—	68	58	59	54	56	58	46

* Courtesy of the Inter-University Consortium for Political Research.

Of even greater interest is the data on party identification. It has been widely assumed in the literature that although voting behavior in contemporary America is heavily influenced by short-term factors of varying kinds, the structure of partisan identification in the electorate has tended to reflect far less change across time. Moreover, the standard work on American voting behavior in the 1950's, *The American Voter,* emphasizes that the voter who is weakly or not at all identified with either major party is less likely to be politically involved or aware than his strongly party-identified compatriot.[29] But during the 1960's, the hitherto glacial measures of party identification have also undergone comparatively abrupt change. As Table 5.7 reveals, there has been a recent and rather sharp increase in independents which has paralleled a sharp decline in the proportion of strong party identifiers—and particularly Democratic Party identifiers—in the electorate.

[28] The percentages are those of the total sample, excluding the categories coded as "don't knows" and "inappropriates." While the 1968 data have not become available in time for inclusion here, the Gallup organization found that only 43 per cent of the 1968 voters chose a straight party ticket, a figure which closely fits the end of this series. See *Gallup Opinion Index,* December 1968, p. 9.

[29] Angus Campbell *et al., The American Voter op. cit.,* pp. 143–45.

Table 5.7 The Decline of Party: Movements in Party
Identification, 1940–1969

Year	Independent	Strong Democratic	Strong Republican	Total Strong Identifiers
1940 *	20			
1944 *	20			
1948 *	19			
1952	23	23	14	37
1956	20	23	16	39
1960	23	21	16	37
1962	22	24	13	37
1964	23	27	11	38
1965 *	23			
1966	29	18	10	28
1967 *	31			
1968	28	23	9	32
1969 *	30			

* AIPO (Gallup) data were used for these years. Figures for the other
years are based on Survey Research Center studies. For the latter, the
three categories of Independent Leaning to Democratic, Independent,
and Independent Leaning to Republican are lumped together.

It is tempting to speculate that the great Democratic collapse of 1966 was a direct outgrowth of the disarray and dis-
illusion arising from the Vietnam war, urban disorders and
the nationalization of the race issue. In any case, the data
reveal a sharp upward shift in independents which can be
pinpointed with some assurance as falling between 1965 and
1966. This shift has apparently resulted in a durable change
in state, with independents moving from one-fifth to nearly
one-third of the total. For what is probably the first time since
reliable survey data became available nearly a generation ago,
the proportion of strong party identifiers in the total electorate
is now no greater than the proportion of independent identifiers.

Moreover, there is some reason for supposing that the nature of political independence may have undergone a profound change since the 1950's. To be sure, the authors of *The American Voter* focus their attention upon individuals in discussing party identifications. Indeed, one lacuna occuring often in the survey literature is the failure to demonstrate a clearly developed relationship between the level of individual attachments to party and what might be described as the "demography" of party identification.[30] But even as dedicated a democrat as the late V. O. Key, Jr. was primarily concerned to show not that independent voters were other than as described in the survey literature, but that independent identifiers and those who switched from party to party in presidential elections were by no means the same voters.[31] There is probably wide consensus that the Survey Research Center view of the independent is the correct one:

> Far from being more attentive, interested and informed, Independents tend as a group to be somewhat less involved in politics. They have somewhat poorer knowledge of the issues, their image of the candidates is fainter, their interest in the campaign is less, their concern over the outcome is relatively slight, and their choice between competing candidates, although it is indeed made later in the campaign, seems much less to spring from discoverable evaluations of the elements of national politics.[32]

There remain a number of imponderables in this question which are beyond the scope of this study to explore in their full detail. One notes from the above evaluation, however, that these are characteristics of relative political unawareness or ignorance. It is well known that, in terms of population groupings, the proportion of "know-nothingness" about our politics tends to be associated with the educationally and economically

[30] Compare, for example, *ibid.*, Chapter 6.
[31] V. O. Key, Jr., *The Responsible Electorate*, pp. 1–28.
[32] Campbell *et al.*, *The American Voter, op. cit.*, p. 143.

deprived, with women more than men, with people under thirty, and with those who live in parts of the country where local tradition and custom have not been favorable to mass participation in partisan electoral politics.

An examination in some detail of party identification as it relates to political response in the 1964 Survey Research Center study presents one side of the problem of the independent in the current decade. The 1964 study, which was made before the recent rapid increase in the independent share of the total electorate, reveals that the demographic and certain other characteristics of independent identifiers do not correspond to what might have been expected. They are clearly not concentrated toward the bottom of the scales of income, occupation, and education; rather to the contrary, in fact. As Table 5.8 reveals, the share of 1964 independents descends with occupational category, and monotonically with income; but along the educational dimension, the peak share of independents falls among high school graduates who have had some college education.

The significant point is that none of the groups among which independents have the largest share (leaving aside categories not discussed as yet, such as southerners or adults under thirty) is the kind of group associated with low political participation or efficacy. If it is indeed true that the profile of the 1964 independent can be read in terms analogous to those used by the authors of *The American Voter,* it would have to follow that there is a rather steep upward gradient in the proportion of individual voters who are political "know-nothings" as one ascends in each social category toward the top of the social scale. But this, if true, would be a significant political anomaly.

The problem is further complicated when one examines certain ranges of political opinion among our party-identified groups. If the Survey Research Center's involvement index is studied, the result is quite clear: independents are indeed dis-

Table 5.8 The Structure of Party Identification, 1964

Category	Number	Strong Dem.	Weak Dem.	Ind.	Weak Rep.	Strong Rep.
Occupation						
Professional-						
Managerial	245	20	21	30	13	16
Clerical-Sales	172	24	25	23	16	12
Skilled, Semi-						
skilled	271	31	24	27	10	8
Unskilled, service	147	41	28	22	8	2
Farmers	44	32	32	9	16	11
Retired, Not Head						
of Household	631	26	26	20	16	12
Income						
$10,000 and Over	309	20	20	26	19	15
$7,500–$9,999	235	23	22	26	18	11
$6,000–$7,499	216	27	30	24	12	7
$4,000–$5,999	305	29	28	21	11	11
Under $4,000	471	33	26	20	11	10
Education						
Grades 0–8	373	39	27	17	11	7
9–11+	302	30	28	23	10	8
High School						
Graduate	329	23	28	23	16	10
High School						
Graduate Plus						
Training	156	21	19	29	16	15
Some College	195	19	21	30	14	16
College Graduate	172	19	21	23	17	20

proportionately concentrated at the lowest end of the scale, particularly by contrast with strong identifiers of either party.[33] On the other hand, a study of the efficacy index—a measure of

[33] Of those with very high and high involvement scores, 54 per cent are strong Democratic or strong Republican Party identifiers, while only 14 per cent are independents. Of those with the lowest involvement scores (those in the three bottom units of the scale), 13 per cent are strong party identifiers, while 38 per cent are independents.

the individual's sense of political competence—reveals an entirely different picture. Among 1964 independents, 36 per cent scored high-to-very-high on this efficacy index, a proportion exceeded only by the 50 per cent of strong Republican identifiers who also had a high-to-very-high score. Of the independents, 37 per cent also scored low-to-very-low on this index, indicating a strongly bimodal distribution for this group; but 36 per cent of strong Democratic identifiers also registered low-to-very-low, while only the strong Republican identifiers had a share of low-efficacy individuals (28 per cent) which was significantly below that of the independents.

Viewing the two groups of strong party identifiers and independents as a whole, the strong Democratic Party identifiers tend to be high in terms of involvement and low on the efficacy scale; the strong Republican identifiers are very high on both; and the independents tend to be markedly low on the involvement continuum, but to have *bimodal* political-efficacy characteristics, with large proportions of both high and low scorers.

Again, on matters related to perceptions of parties and behavior in the electoral context of 1964, independents clearly showed evidence of lesser involvement—indeed, of much lesser involvement—than the strong identifiers with the two major parties. Thus, while 76 per cent of the strong Democrats and 84 per cent of the strong Republicans in the sample claimed to have cast ballots for one or the other of the major candidates, only 62 per cent of the independents claimed to have done so. Similarly, favorable references to either party were, of course, much scarcer among independents than among either weak or strong party identifiers: 63 per cent had no positive response to make concerning the Democrats (compared with 19 per cent among strong identifiers), while 75 per cent had no favorable references to make about the Republicans (compared with 20 per cent among strong identifiers). On the other hand, the structure of opinions on two key issues and on the generalized question of the threat of growing governmental power reveals very little difference between the independents and any of the other four categories of identifiers, with the conspicuous exception of strong Republicans. Responses on the three questions are provided in Table 5.9. As is evident, independents show up rather well on the "don't know" category in all three questions when compared with all other groups except the highly politically conscious and involved, though relatively small, group of strong Republicans. Except on the question of help to Negroes, their general policy attitudes tend to fall in the middle, as one might expect.

The conclusion of this part of the study must remain ambiguous. It is evident enough that the 1964 independents show less

Table 5.9 Party Identification and Issue Questions, 1964

Response	Number	Strong Dem.	Weak Dem.	Ind.	Weak Rep.	Strong Rep.
A. *Is the (federal) government getting too powerful?*						
Yes	468	16	24	30	43	66
Depends	49	3	3	5	2	2
No	554	49	39	35	25	15
Don't Know, No Interest	465	32	34	30	30	17
B. *Do you favor Medicare?*						
Yes	763	66	54	47	35	22
Depends	94	6	4	6	7	8
No	435	12	24	30	39	62
Don't Know, No Interest	244	15	17	17	19	8
C. *Do you favor government help to Negroes who can't find jobs?*						
Yes, Favor	596	50	35	43	31	19
Depends	114	6	6	7	11	9
Leave to States	618	33	41	36	44	63
Don't Know, No Interest	205	11	18	13	15	9

awareness of and involvement in the existing instrumentalities of electoral politics than do party identifiers. But it is equally clear that there is some kind of bimodality in operation in their demographic profile: one finds small but suggestive tendencies to peak among both professional-managerial *and* skilled-semi-skilled occupations, for instance; among self-identified (or "class-conscious") members of the middle class, but *also* among nonself-identified (or relatively not "class-conscious") working-class people; and toward the top, but not at the very top, of the educational scale. It is also clear that independents tend to split between those with high-to-very-high scores of political efficacy and those with low-to-very-low scores.

To note all this is not necessarily an attempt to demonstrate that independents are more politically conscious, at least during this decade, than those examined in *The American Voter* but only to make clear that there seem to be significant discrepancies in the data. It may be entirely likely that there are at least *two* sets of independents: "old independents" who correspond to the rather bleak classical survey-research picture, and "new independents" who may have declined to identify with either major party not because they are relatively politically unconscious, but because the structure of electoral politics at the present time turns upon parties, issues, and symbolisms which do not have much meaning in terms of their political values or cognitions.

These considerations bring us to the second aspect of the problem of independent identification: the steep post-1965 increase to a new level and, associated with this, the structure of these increases. If one compares the June 1965 Gallup survey with that of September 1967, when the proportion of independents reached what seems to be about its present level, it seems clear that the increase has been most heavily concentrated among those population groups where—barring a highly improbable distribution of individual voters—one would least expect to find disproportionate shares of the politically incompetent or the politically unaware. The array of increases is presented both for its minimum and maximum in Table 5.10. The evidence seems strong, though not necessarily overwhelming, that the recent decline in Democratic identification and increase in independent adults is concentrated toward the top of the social structure, precisely where one might expect to find the most stable linkages between voters and existing party and other political structures. Not only the increase but the absolute proportion of independents has become increasingly identified with the comfortable urban-suburban middle class.

One further aspect of the political independent requires discussion: the fact that this characteristic is so high among young adults. If systematic change is occurring in the direction of ero-

Table 5.10 Growth of the "New Independent": Shifts in Proportion of Independents by Social Category, June 1965–September 1967 *

Category	Increase
Age 30–49	11
Highest Income ($7,000 and Over)	10
College Educated	10
Nonwhite	10
Age 21–29	10
White-Collar Occupations	10
U.S.	8
Age 50 and Over	6
Women	6
Grade-School Education	5
Middle Income ($5,000–$6,999)	5
Low Income (Under $3,000)	3
Farmers	2

* Based on published AIPO (Gallup) data.

sion in party linkages among the youngest age cohorts, the long-range implications are likely to be profound. To be sure, this is a group which is the least politically socialized of any age-stratified group in the electorate; mobility is apt to be considerably greater than it will be later, social roles are not as fixed as they subsequently become, and so on. This is reflected in the data, and along two dimensions. Taking the Gallup surveys of party affiliation from 1951 through 1968, voters in the twenty-one to twenty-nine age group had a larger share of independents than either the thirty to forty-nine age group or voters over fifty in each survey; and in each survey the proportion of independents fell monotonically from the youngest to the oldest group. Secondly, the variations over time are also monotonically arrayed: greatest among the twenty-one to twenty-nine-year-olds (standard deviation: 5.0), next among voters aged thirty to forty-nine (standard deviation: 3.4), and least among those fifty or over (standard deviation: 2.8).[34]

At the same time, the stratification pattern among young voters bears some similarity to that found in the larger population. The most significant of these differences is the far greater proportion of independents among whites (42 per cent) than among nonwhites (24 per cent); among men (44 per cent) as compared with women (37 per cent); and as between those with a college education (44 per cent) and those with high school (39 per cent) or grade school (38 per cent) educations. Moreover, the "generation gap" has clearly widened: while in 1965 the difference between the proportion of independents among the youngest and oldest age classes was 12 per cent, this widened in 1967–68 to 16 per cent, the largest spread in this seventeen-year series. As one reaches college students in this analysis, the proportion of independents rises to a global total of 44 per cent in early 1969, and to 53 per cent by the

[34] *Gallup Opinion Index,* June 1968, p. 2.

end of the year.[35] Here there is a typical downward movement with age and school class.

Of much higher salience, however, is the very strong positive relationship between political and social radicalism and
lack of party affiliation: while only 23 per cent of students
classifying themselves as "extremely conservative" are independents, the proportion rises steadily to a whopping 57 per cent
among those describing themselves as "extremely liberal."
While those students who have struck to the conventional col-
legiate dissipation—getting drunk on occasion—have an independent proportion nearly identical with that of college students as a whole (45 per cent), those who have explored the
drug scene score much higher: 60 per cent among those who
have tried marijuana, 65 per cent among those who have tried
barbiturates, and 82 per cent among those who have experi-
mented with LSD.

While a summary of all of these findings must remain ambiguous until further intensive work is done, the pattern of
change in recent years seems fairly clear. The political parties
are progressively losing their hold upon the electorate. A new
breed of independent seems to be emerging as well—a person
with a better-than-average education, making a better-than-
average income in a better-than-average occupation, and, very
possibly, a person whose political cognitions and awareness
keep him from making identifications with either old party.
The losses the two parties, particularly the Democrats, have
suffered in this decade have largely been concentrated among
precisely those strata in the population most likely to act
through and in the political system out of proportion to their
numbers. This may point toward the progressive dissolution of
the parties as action intermediaries in electoral choice and
other politically relevant acts. It may also be indicative of the

[35] *Ibid.*, June 1969, p. 39; Jan. 1970, p. 14.

production of a mass base for independent political movements of ideological tone and considerable long-term staying power.[36]

What are the policy implications of these movements toward electoral disaggregation? There is every reason to suppose that twentieth-century American politics has been pre-eminently marked by the decomposition and contraction of those partisan structures and functions which reached their widest, most cohesive form in the decades after the Civil War. This decomposition alone is enough to set the evolution of American electoral politics apart as something approaching the unique in the Western world, not least because its origins can be traced back so far in time. That is, it can be traced back to the time when the centralist imperatives of order and control implicit in mature industrial capitalism came more and more into collision with a pre-existing, fully mobilized party system of preindustrial origin. The "classical" American response to this confrontation was, after all, the partial destruction of these nineteenth-century partisan linkages.

Of course, the New Deal era was a time in which political power was reallocated, shifting somewhat from the hands of the business elite and its political ancillaries to a more pluralist, welfare-oriented coalition of elites and veto groups. This was the minimum price, in all probability, of system survival. To that extent, parties resumed a good deal of their former importance as *instruments of collective social action*. This meant that not only the identity of individual office holders

[36] Here the Gallup survey is once again of interest. As of October 1968 (*Gallup Opinion Index*, October 1968, p. 27), 27 per cent of American voters wished to see the establishment of a new political party whose principles are more in line with their views than either of the two major parties, while 67 per cent expressed satisfaction with the status quo. The familiar loading occurs: the more deprived strata are less interested than the upper-middle strata, the South is somewhat disproportionately favorable to a new party (31 per cent), and fully 41 per cent of independent identifiers favor the idea, compared with 52 per cent of independents who favor the existing partisan order.

and the distribution of symbolic benefits but their role as a significant influence over the contours of public policy were at stake.

But while it was possible for traditional American governmental structures and the dominant American political formula to survive and adapt to the transition from business rule to disaggregated welfarism, it was—and has remained—considerably less clear that further major democratic adaptations to the collective pressures of mature industrialism could be achieved without the gravest cultural and institutional transformations. It seems evident in retrospect that the policy choices which even the New Dealers made in their heyday tended to fall short of radical innovation.[37]

Moreover, while quantitative indices support the qualitative judgment that party as an instrument of broadly national, collective initiatives was restored during the 1932–48 period, at no time during that period did new organizational forms of party emerge. Such forms might have served as a crystallized, action-oriented definition of party as an open system of action in which the many who were individually powerless could pursue collective political objectives under elites identified with them. But they did not, and it seems very likely that under American conditions, even at the height of the Great Depression, they could not. Mass voting behavior was transformed enormously during the 1930's; partisan organization and processes seem scarcely to have changed at all.

Moreover, the post-1952 resumption of the march toward electoral disaggregation leads one to suspect the possibility that, in terms of the history of American voting behavior at least, the New Deal might come to be regarded one day as a

[37] For a useful comparative discussion of this and many other matters of interest to American political scientists, including a review of the genesis of the Social Security Act, see Andrew Shonfield, *Modern Capitalism* (New York: Oxford University Press, 1965), pp. 298–329.

temporary if massive deviation from a secular trend toward the gradual disappearance of the political party in the United States. It is clear that the significance of the party as an intermediary link between voters and rulers has again come into serious question. Bathed in the warm glow of diffused affluence, vexed in spirit but enriched economically by our imperial military and space commitments, confronted by the gradually unfolding consequences of social change as vast as it is unplanned, what need have Americans of political parties? More precisely, what need have they of parties whose structures, processes, and leadership cadres find their origins in a past as remote as it is irrelevant?

It seems fairly evident that if this secular trend toward politics without parties continues to unfold, the policy consequences will be profound. To state the matter with utmost simplicity: political parties, with all their well-known human and structural shortcomings, are the only devices thus far invented by the wit of Western man which with some effectiveness can generate countervailing collective power on behalf of the many individually powerless against the relatively few who are individually—or organizationally—powerful. Their disappearance could only entail the unchallenged ascendancy of the latter unless new structures of collective power were developed to replace them and unless conditions in the social structure and the political culture were such that they could be effectively used. This contingency, despite recent publicity for the term "participatory democracy," seems precisely what is not likely to occur under at least immediately conceivable circumstances in the United States. Assuming that it does not, the policies of a politics without parties would certainly not be overtly similar in any detail to those of the 1920's. As American political and economic elites have learned to accept and use Keynesian economics to their and the country's profit, so they have learned to accept, and profit from, the disaggregated welfarism which was the political legacy of the New Deal era. Within those limits, however, there would be little reason to doubt that public policy would generally tend to be as system-maintaining or "conservative" for its time as was that of the 1920's for that time, even though punctuated from time to time by fire-brigade rescue operations.

6

The Contemporary Scene II: An Emergent Realignment?

Thus far we have presented evidence for one set of political trends which have been hallmarks of American politics during the 1960's. But there is also considerable evidence that this country is now in a realigning sequence and that we are en route to a sixth party system. Critical realignments, as we have argued, arise out of increasingly visible social maladjustments; these in turn are the product of dynamic transformations in a quite separately developing socioeconomic system. Such transformations entail the emergence of quite unevenly distributed social costs. Some sectors of society are injured or threatened with injury far more directly than others, and eventually the pressure upon them produces stress which makes them particularly available for political mobilization by third parties or for subsequent massive shifts from one major party's following to the other's.

Were the American policy structure or the integrative machinery of the two major party organizations equipped to take at least an intermediate-range view of socioeconomic trans- formations and the protests of injured groups before a flash point had been reached, it is possible that the phenomenon of critical realignment would be much more infrequent than it has been, and very likely that in any event it would not have its peculiar property of periodic recurrence. But this would be to presuppose a political system which does not exist in the United States. As far as the pluralist and dispersed policy structure is concerned, there is every practical motivation for dealing with problems as they arise and as they are presented by already-organized shared-interest groups. In the absence of cohesive majorities and confronted by the enormously com- plex sequence of policy-making from the initial presentation of political demands to final disposition, policymakers are con- strained both by their consensual liberal-pluralist ideology and by lack of time to take a short-range view. Thus demands are dealt with only when they have become so intense that it no longer seems safe to defer them any longer.

Similar considerations engage the attention of the leaders and managers of party and organizations. They manage hetero- geneous coalitions, many of whose subgroups are only slightly less hostile to each other and their goals than to groups identi- fied with the opposition. They are not well equipped, either in ideology or in incentives, to incorporate discordant demands arising from newly mobilized groups. They are particularly ill- equipped to deal with emergent demand which cannot be mor- selized, or broken down into piecemeal claims which can be met by marginal changes in welfare or other policy outputs. If, as Theodore J. Lowi has argued, it is always easier in this political system to formulate distributive policies than redis- tributive ones—that, for example, it was easier to reach agree- ment on tariff schedules in the old days than on major changes in the tax laws today—it is equally true that the parties' coalition managers are overwhelmingly preoccupied with achieving a balance of subcoalitional tensions which will permit them to win elections in the short run.

It can be taken as a necessary consequence of the realities of incremental bargaining politics in the United States that they will tend to produce crises which lead to nonincremental change. In the interim, this change will be associated, as it has been in every realigning sequence, with that sharp increase in the political temperature which occurs when groups adopt absolutist value (or value-cum-interest) positions which at least temporarily make bargaining impossible.

If one is to contemplate realignment in the contemporary period, it is essential to identify the most important emergent demands on the system arising from change-induced dislocations in the society and in the economy. It is probably particularly important to identify the possible sources of *countermobilization*, for realigning sequences seem typically to involve waves of mobilization: a mobilization of protest against the existing structure of politics is followed by a countermobilization of groups hostile to and threatened by these new demands for redefinitions of social allocations through political means. In the present era, these sources of protest and counterprotest can be quite clearly, if generally, identified. As was so often true in the past, they also interact with each other. They are:

1. The massive but uneven spread of material affluence.

2. The tendency of the social structure to be transformed under the pressure of the postwar technological explosion from the classical capitalist stratification pattern—owners, middle classes, working classes, farmers—into a pattern made up of those who can be classified in David Apter's terms as technologically competent, technologically obsolescent, and techno-

logically superfluous.[1]

3. One of the great population transfers of modern times, the result of which has been to move large parts of the southern rural proletariat—particularly the black proletariat—from the countryside into the central cities, which are also the nerve centers of the economic and social system.

The first of these developments in the socioeconomic system has so far been channeled and regulated by federal governmental policy, and has in no small measure been stabilized by the development of public-sector spending by the military establishment. Of course, it is true that a rapidly expanding economic base should, all other things being equal, make the task of policymakers easier by eliminating bitter Malthusian group conflict over allocations of scarce resources. Indeed, this development of affluence was one of the preconditions for the argument so fashionable among pluralist social scientists until very recently that an "end of ideology" and a golden age of political consensus were in the offing. It was perhaps not adequately realized by such analysts that this affluence was unevenly distributed, that it severely but again unevenly eroded traditional American economic motivations which form a major part of the dominant Lockian political ideology—particularly among the "children of affluence" in the universities; and that it stimulated expectations among certain groups, most notably the black population in the cities, which could only be satisfied by relatively drastic changes in policy outputs and, very possibly, in the political structure itself.

Associated with this uneven but sweeping transition to affluence is an emergent reorganization of American patterns of social stratification. The old and familiar industrial stratification pattern—upper, middle, and working classes—is now be-

[1] See David Apter's essay, "Ideology and Discontent," in David Apter (ed.), *Ideology and Discontent* (Glencoe, Ill.: The Free Press, 1964), pp. 15–43.

coming supplanted by one which is relevant to a system dominated by advanced postindustrial technology. As Apter argues, one of the major consequences of this transition has been the development of a professional-managerial-technical elite (Apter's "technologically competent"). This elite is closely connected with the universities and research centers, and significant parts of it have been drawn—both out of ideology and interest—to the federal government's domestic social activism during the past decade. It tends to be more politically cosmopolitan and socially permissive than does the society as a whole; and it is undergoing long-range relative growth.

At the bottom of this stratification model is a stratum, also growing, of people whom Apter has termed "technologically superfluous," whose economic functions have been undermined or terminated by the technological revolution of the past generation. These are the people, white and black, who tend to be in the hard-core poverty areas. They were the subjects of Michael Harrington's *The Other America* a decade ago, and of the federal government's poverty programs since; and, for considerable portions of the new technological, cosmopolitan elite they form clients and natural political allies.

In between these two growing sectors, subjected to cultural and political pressure from both and perceiving itself to be declining in cultural influence and political significance, is what has recently been termed "the great middle" or "middle America"—an aggregation of Apter's "technologically obsolescent"—mixed no doubt with other elements—and concentrated among older local elites, white-collar employees and white production workers. These are today the chief carriers and defenders of the old American middle-class dream and its associated values.

It is evident that a model worded as broadly as this can leave out much important detail, assuming that even the broad picture has some validity. It hardly needs saying that, as previous orderings of American society tended in actuality to be heterogeneous coalitions rather than large monoliths separated by great chasms, such an emergent stratification would also be heterogeneous. At the same time, major reorganizations of the American social structure seem to have underlain every era of critical realignment in the past. They have produced cumulative strains on social and political consensus, and, consequently, new types and intensities of political oppositions which eventually need only a sudden increase in stress to release a denotation extending to the furthest reaches of the political system. It is clear that were an emergent transformation in American social structure of the general type outlined above to achieve political relevance under sufficiently stressful conditions, political front lines would be drawn in entirely new places; the trenches which so clearly marked the boundaries between the parties under the order established in the 1930's would rapidly become deserted and useless.

Reorganizations of what might be called politically relevant patterns of social structure have almost always produced not only economic and status conflict, but—in greater or lesser degree—profound cultural polarizations as well. One is increasingly inclined to suspect that locally based cultural hatreds overwhelmingly dominated the intense political climates of all realigning eras except for the New Deal sequence, where economic issues were of exceptional salience. Even here, one needs merely to reread Samuel Lubell's classic *The Future of American Politics* [2] to perceive that group animosities—often having little directly to do with economic issues but much to do with cultural conflict—continued to flourish vigorously even then.

The struggle between discrete, mobilized, and antagonistic groups cannot be satisfactorily settled in liberal-pluralist terms or through liberal-pluralistic political institutions. They may, if they are not too intense or if the groups are small

[2] New York: Harper, 1952.

enough, be "institutionalized" through strong identification by one group with the party which is seen to be the enemy of the other; they may gradually wither away; or they may escalate to the point of civil war, genocide, or an imposed dictatorship over the one "side" and its groups by the other "side." So long as these cultural struggles are intense "world-view" conflicts, there is one thing that cannot be done with them: they cannot be treated in a "more or less" fashion by the policy machinery, as though they were equivalent to conflicts over tariffs, taxes, or minimum wages. They inherently involve not questions of more or less, but of either-or.

There is a good deal of evidence, some of which we shall examine in this chapter, that the past few years have been marked by a redefinition of American politics in which the alliance between the top and bottom of the new stratification pattern has become increasingly met by countermobilization within the threatened middle. The old American value consensus has been supplanted by dissent and the emergence of new life styles and motivations on one side, and by anxious but intense reaffirmations on the other. Kevin Phillips, himself a spokesman for these threatened middle strata in an administration of spokesmen for them, has persuasively argued that this countermobilization is destined to produce an emergent Republican majority and a sixth party system constructed in a very different way than was the New Deal system.[3] This remains to be seen. It is particularly doubtful, for reasons which are discussed at length in this book, that a new majority would be "Republican" in any well-defined, party-identified sense of the term; but such a majority, if derived from the "great middle," would surely be profoundly conservative, if not reactionary, and it would be based upon an intensity of polarized cultural conflict which is already a conspicuous part of the

[3] Kevin Phillips, *The Emergent Republican Majority* (New York: Arlington, 1969).

current American political scene.

Here, of course, the third great unplanned, uncontrolled transformation is of the greatest relevance: the tremendous migration of rural southerners, particularly of Negroes, into our major cities. This has nationalized the racial polarity and hostility which has long been a hallmark of the South. George Wallace was the first political enterpreneur who perceived this reality and acted upon it, in the process becoming a figure of national significance and quite possibly a portent of things to come. This nationalization has had several consequences: it has destroyed the old bases of the Democratic party in most of the South, at least for the time being; it has helped motivate blacks to develop a greater sense of their own political identity as a separate quasinational group in the United States; and it has led to ferocious countermobilization by those whites of the "great middle" who are least able to escape the black presence by flight into the suburbs or to private schools for their children.

The discordance which has been developing along these lines was admirably captured in two major events of 1968—the Democratic convention in August, and the election itself in November. If it is indeed true that the deviations from the norms of American politics in 1968 are part of a critical realignment, they would have to be viewed as an intermediate stage in a larger disruption, the initial manifestation of which might well prove to be the remarkable showing made by George Wallace in the Democratic presidential primaries during the spring of 1964. It is also very evident that the 1964 election itself constituted a remarkable break with the past, involving precisely the sharp, visible transformation of party images which has been associated with earlier realignments.[4]

The most durable consequence of this election may prove to

[4] Cf. Walter Dean Burnham, "American Voting Behavior and the 1964 Election," *op. cit.*

be the Republicans' "southern strategy," which was self-consciously played out by the Goldwater coalition's leaders in 1964 and has had dramatic consequences for the alignment of party support in the South. This strategy was employed again by the Nixon coalition in 1968, although in far more modulated form and with the appeal aimed at the Southern "rimland" and border states rather than at the Deep South core where the region's politics of race has been most uninhibited. It appears to remain very much on the Nixon Administration's agenda, as both major parties attempt to redefine their coalitional base in a highly fluid period. That a party which for almost a century had no usable southern base of support would undertake such policies is in itself indicative of a transition to an alignment based to a substantial extent on race and section, even without the added impact of the intervening Wallace phenomenon.

The Wallace movement of 1968 falls almost too easily into the historical pattern of abnormal phenomena associated with the early stages of critical realignment. It is, in the first place, not a product of a major party bolt, as were the Roosevelt progressives of 1912, for example, but has its roots outside of the old major-party structure. Second, it is a *movement:* its leaders are concerned with the future rather than with immediate electoral success, and are dedicated to producing a popular uprising against the conspiracy of top political elites, intellectuals, blacks, and others against the "common man." [5] Third, it is of very large aggregate size: the 13.6 per cent of the three-party vote which Wallace won in 1968 was exceeded during the past century only by La Follette's 16.7 per cent of the 1924 three-party vote. Of course, the mass base of the Wallace movement is heavily concentrated in the South: 51.3 per cent of his vote was cast in the ex-Confederate states, compared with 14.6 per cent of Humphrey's and 16.1 per cent of

[5] For a good description of the Wallace *ambiance,* see Marshall Frady, *Wallace* (New York: World Publishing, 1968).

Nixon's. But even outside the South, Wallace's appeal was considerable: 8.3 per cent of the total, which during the past century was exceeded by La Follette (17.8 per cent) but not, significantly, by the Populists of 1892 (7.1 per cent). Finally, the Wallace movement, like its predecessors, has a heavily rural and anticosmopolitan tinge in its southern heartland. A ranking of Wallace's share of the vote in the ex-Confederacy, in Table 6.1, partitioning the area between the five Deep South states which Goldwater carried in 1964 and the six rimland states, and by three categories of urbanization, makes the point with great clarity.

Within the behavioral constraints which require partitioning the South into two subregions, Wallace's appeal in each subregion—and in each state in both subregions—is clearly great-

Table 6.1   The 1968 Vote in the South and the Nation *

Category	% Dem.	% Rep.	% Wallace
Deep South: Nonmetropolitan	23.2	20.0	56.8
Deep South: Metropolitan Areas Under 300,000	26.5	31.3	42.2
Deep South: Metropolitan Areas of 300,000 and Over	32.7	28.9	38.4
Rim South: Nonmetropolitan	30.5	37.9	31.6
Rim South: Metropolitan Areas Under 300,000	32.3	43.8	23.9
Rim South: Metropolitan Areas of 300,000 and Over	38.8	40.3	20.9
Deep South: Total	25.3	24.0	50.8
Rim South: Total	33.6	39.6	26.7
Non-South: Total	45.9	45.8	8.3
United States: Total	42.9	43.6	13.6

* Percentages are of the three-party vote; when totaled, they may slightly exceed 100 because of the rounding necessary in a three-party contest.

est in the rural and small-town areas and declines markedly
as one approaches the larger metropolitan centers. Evidently
the largest southern city which Wallace carried—after Bir-
mingham and Mobile in his native Alabama—was Jackson-
ville, Florida, which ranks fifteenth among the cities of the
region. This distribution of third-party strength is hardly a
surprise. The Wallace campaign was organized around neo-
populist themes: in addition to the racism which was at its
center, it emphasized hostility to the "centers" of American
life—the federal government, intellectuals, and urban-cosmo-
politan liberalism. The structure of the southern vote in November underscores Wallace's periphery-oriented appeal and,
indeed, establishes a peculiar link with mass-based third-party
"movements" in the American past.

Outside the South, the distribution of Wallace's strength becomes much less visibly a matter of distance from central cities
or from the cosmopolitan heartlands of the country. His appeal
was to the "little people"—white, of course—who are caught
up in the pressures produced by our contemporary social transformations and who have neither the material resources nor the
psychological security to evade the confrontation, as members
of the more comfortable classes do. We will not attempt an
exhaustive evaluation of Wallace's electoral strength and weaknesses throughout the nonsouthern regions of the country, but
we will examine the structuring of the Wallace vote in two
areas of the Northeast: Baltimore, Maryland, and Delaware
County, Pennsylvania. Wallace's penetration of the electorate
was somewhat above the nonsouthern average in both cases—
about 15 per cent of the white electorate in Baltimore, and 9.5
per cent of the three-party vote in Delaware County. It is not
difficult to obtain from both cases very strong evidence that
such a phenomenon as "urban populism" exists, that it affects
some strata of the population far more profoundly than others,
and that—in these communities, at least—Wallace's support

was drawn disproportionately from parts of the white population which were once predominantly Democratic in their voting behavior. It is also not difficult—particularly in the case of Baltimore—to detect persuasive evidence of an upper- to middle-class white electoral alliance with the black electorate against the "broad middle" in between whenever candidacies involving racial hostilities and "urban populism" emerge.

Delaware County is a cluster of forty-nine suburban communities which form part of the Philadelphia metropolitan area. These communities have a very wide range of occupational stratification, income, and distribution in both the "normal" partisan vote and in the magnitude of Wallace's penetration in 1968. The county, however, is overwhelmingly white; as of 1960 only one of its subdivisions had a black majority, and in only four others did the nonwhite population exceed a quarter of the total. The industrial areas of the county tend to be concentrated along the Delaware River, as does a large part of the working class and the core of "traditional" Democratic support. Similarly, the upland areas in the central and western parts of the county tend strongly to be middle to upper class, residential, and Republican.

Table 6.2 Correlates of Voting Behavior 1960–1968: The Case of Delaware County, Pennsylvania

1960 Census Classification	% Dem. 1960	% Dem. 1964	% Dem. 1968	% Rep. 1968	% Wallace 1968
% Professional-Managerial	−.743	−.597	−.483	+.786	−.795
% Clerical-Sales	−.110	−.119	+.070	+.235	−.567
% Skilled and Semi-skilled	+.657	+.472	+.369	−.736	+.872
% Unskilled and Service	+.179	+.287	+.132	−.166	+.123
% Foreign-Stock White	+.439	+.427	+.434	−.247	−.227
1959 Income (Families)	−.683	−.579	−.582	+.699	−.621

A correlation of the percentages cast for the major parties in presidential elections since 1960 with the most salient measurable demographic characteristics (Table 6.2) sharply pinpoints both the more traditional pattern and that of 1968.

Wallace's appeal is very strongly and positively correlated with the percentage of skilled and semiskilled blue-collar workers in the population. Since 1960 there has been a steep decline in class polarization as associated with the Democratic vote, but not as associated with the Republican vote; this seems another way of suggesting that Change Wallace won a far greater share of ex-Democratic votes than of ex-Republican ones. (See also Maps 6.1–6.3) Similarly, the profile of the Wallace correlations closely resembles that of the Kennedy correlations of 1960, except for the clerical-sales and foreign-stock categories. The negative correlation between the percentage for Wallace and the foreign-stock percentage of 1960, while small, conveys the impression that his appeal also was differentially greater among native-stock elements, a finding which is confirmed in the Baltimore data. With this profile is associated a positive correlation of +.503 between the Democratic vote of 1960 and the Wallace vote of 1968.

The quantitative magnitude of these movements is indicated by Table 6.3.

It is clear from Tables 6.2 and 6.3 that the 1964 election was part of a transitional movement away from the older alignment pattern. It was peculiarly marked by severe reduction of polarization along class lines by comparison with 1960, a reduction which resulted from abnormally large pro-Democratic movements among upper- and upper-middle-class areas, and abnormally small ones among the blue-collar townships and boroughs of this county. Thus the average standard deviation of the percentages in the four categories of Table 6.3 declines from 10 in 1960 to 5.74 in 1964. Similarly, the Wallace correlation with the 1964 Democratic vote drops to +.319 but is nega-

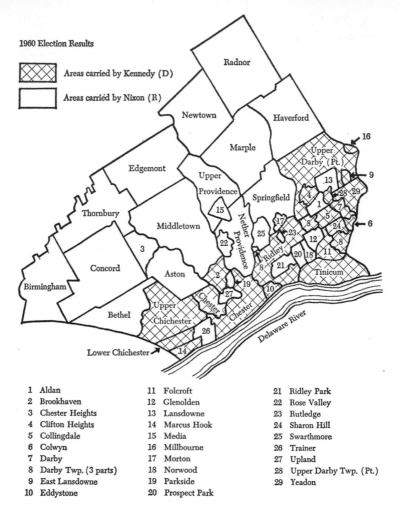

1960 Election Results

Areas carried by Kennedy (D)

Areas carried by Nixon (R)

1	Aldan	11	Folcroft	21	Ridley Park
2	Brookhaven	12	Glenolden	22	Rose Valley
3	Chester Heights	13	Lansdowne	23	Rutledge
4	Clifton Heights	14	Marcus Hook	24	Sharon Hill
5	Collingdale	15	Media	25	Swarthmore
6	Colwyn	16	Millbourne	26	Trainer
7	Darby	17	Morton	27	Upland
8	Darby Twp. (3 parts)	18	Norwood	28	Upper Darby Twp. (Pt.)
9	East Lansdowne	19	Parkside	29	Yeadon
10	Eddystone	20	Prospect Park		

Map 6.1 The Outcome of the 1960 Election in Delaware County, Pennsylvania

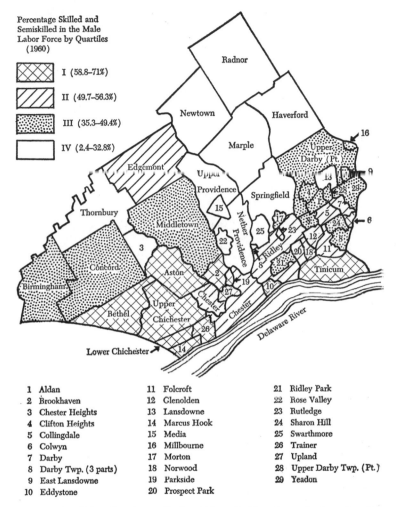

Percentage Skilled and
Semiskilled in the Male
Labor Force by Quartiles
(1960)

I (58.8–71%)

II (49.7–56.3%)

III (35.3–49.4%)

IV (2.4–32.8%)

1	Aldan	11	Folcroft	21	Ridley Park
2	Brookhaven	12	Glenolden	22	Rose Valley
3	Chester Heights	13	Lansdowne	23	Rutledge
4	Clifton Heights	14	Marcus Hook	24	Sharon Hill
5	Collingdale	15	Media	25	Swarthmore
6	Colwyn	16	Millbourne	26	Trainer
7	Darby	17	Morton	27	Upland
8	Darby Twp. (3 parts)	18	Norwood	28	Upper Darby Twp. (Pt.)
9	East Lansdowne	19	Parkside	29	Yeadon
10	Eddystone	20	Prospect Park		

Map 6.2 Distribution of the Blue-Collar Population in the Suburbs: The Case of Delaware County

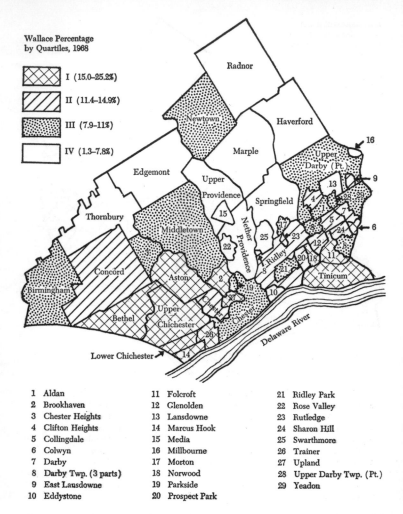

Map 6.3 **Sources of Support for the Wallace Movement, 1968: The Case of Delaware County**

Wallace Percentage
by Quartiles, 1968

I (15.0–25.2%)
II (11.4–14.9%)
III (7.9–11%)
IV (1.3–7.8%)

1 Aldan	11 Folcroft	21 Ridley Park
2 Brookhaven	12 Glenolden	22 Rose Valley
3 Chester Heights	13 Lansdowne	23 Rutledge
4 Clifton Heights	14 Marcus Hook	24 Sharon Hill
5 Collingdale	15 Media	25 Swarthmore
6 Colwyn	16 Millbourne	26 Trainer
7 Darby	17 Morton	27 Upland
8 Darby Twp. (3 parts)	18 Norwood	28 Upper Darby Twp. (Pt.)
9 East Lansdowne	19 Parkside	29 Yeadon
10 Eddystone	20 Prospect Park	

Table 6.3 Class Dimensions of Voting Behavior in Delaware County, 1960–1968

Percentage Skilled and Semiskilled of 1960 Male Labor Force	Number	Means					
		% Dem. 1960	% Dem. 1964	% Dem. 1968	% Rep. 1968	% Wallace 1968	Dem. Defection Ratio, 1964–1968
0–29.9	12	32.4	49.0	33.0	61.4	5.6	32.6
30–49.9	15	45.7	56.0	39.1	51.0	9.9	30.2
50–59.9	14	52.0	57.1	39.4	44.3	16.3	31.0
60 and Over	7	54.9	63.0	42.2	40.6	17.3	33.0

Percentage Skilled and Semiskilled of 1960 Male Labor Force	Number	Standard Deviations				
		% Dem. 1960	% Dem. 1964	% Dem. 1968	% Rep. 1968	% Wallace 1968
0–29.9	12	7.82	3.59	5.31	5.21	2.84
30–49.9	15	14.07	11.29	11.61	11.38	2.07
50–59.9	14	11.41	8.21	7.27	6.23	3.39
60 and Over	7	6.67	6.63	4.04	5.31	5.19

tively, and rather strongly, associated with the magnitude of
the 1960–64 Democratic shift (−527).

The Johnson coalition, as both Tables 6.2 and 6.3 make
clear, fell apart in two directions in this suburban county.
There is an extraordinary uniformity in the Democratic defection ratio among the four class categories of Table 6.3. Similarly, the standard deviation of the Democratic percentages
among these categories continues to fall from 5.74 in 1964 to
3.88 in 1968. The Republican standard deviation, on the other
hand, returns at 9.13 nearly to the 1960 level. It is obvious that
while upper-strata areas returned for the most part to their
traditional Republican allegiance once the negative stimulus
of the Goldwater candidacy was removed, the breakaway from
the Democrats among blue-collar areas was overwhelmingly
toward Wallace. The net result in 1968 was to produce both a
remarkably uniform Democratic defection ratio and a class
homogeneity in the Democratic percentage unprecedented
since the 1928–36 realignment. On the other hand, class stratification returned to its former salience in the Republican vote
and was quite conspicuous in the Wallace vote as well. More
than a few traces of "urban populism" can thus be found in
the structure of the 1968 vote in Delaware county.

If one turns to the structure of recent voting in Baltimore,
much the same pattern can be detected, as shown in Table 6.4.
Here, because of the easy accessibility of precinct returns, it
is possible to construct eighty-three political areas of the city
which are comparable with census areas. In Baltimore, unlike
Delaware County, there is a very large black electorate, a
point which should be borne in mind when examining these
simple correlation coefficients. Even so, it is evident not only
that the Wallace vote tends to correspond to the same general
pattern found in Delaware County, but that there have been
some marvelous transformations in the bases of electoral support within Baltimore during the last decade. The Democratic
nomination for governor in 1966 was won by George Mahoney,

Table 6.4 Correlates of Voting Behavior, 1960–1968:
The Case of Baltimore

1960 Census and Political Classification	% Democratic			
	1960	1962	1964	1966
% Democratic 1960	1.000	+.779	+.837	−.172
% Democratic 1962	+.779	1.000	+.427	+.337
% Democratic 1964	+.837	+.427	1.000	−.635
% Democratic 1966 (of 3-party vote)	.170	.007	.695	1.000
% Democratic 1968	+.681	+.210	+.946	−.783
% Republican 1968	−.838	−.473	−.968	−.551
% Wallace 1968	−.014	+.464	−.449	+.917
% Nonwhite	+.537	+.081	+.824	−.729
% Foreign-Stock White	−.096	+.048	−.327	+.320
% Professional-Managerial	−.694	−.622	−.571	−.072
% Clerical-Sales	−.526	−.416	−.521	+.098
% Skilled and Semiskilled	+.384	+.584	+.078	+.539
% Unskilled and Service	+.611	+.324	+.739	−.418

1960 Census and Political Classification	% Dem. 1968	% Rep. 1968	% Wallace 1968
% Democratic 1960	+.681	−.838	−.014
% Democratic 1962	+.210	−.473	+.464
% Democratic 1964	+.946	−.968	−.449
% Democratic 1966 (of 3-party vote)	−.783	−.551	+.917
% Democratic 1968	1.000	−.937	−.652
% Republican 1968	−.937	1.000	+.350
% Wallace 1968	−.652	+.350	1.000
% Nonwhite	+.830	−.765	−.569
% Foreign-Stock White	−.312	+.311	+.169
% Professional-Managerial	−.418	+.625	−.234
% Clerical-Sales	−.391	+.511	−.061
% Skilled and Semiskilled	−.094	−.180	+.640
% Unskilled and Service	+.670	−.705	−.268

a perennial candidate who on this occasion constructed his appeal on grounds very similar to Wallace's in 1968. The correlation of +.917 between Mahoney's vote and Wallace's suggests precisely this, as does the comparability of their correlation profiles generally. To see more clearly the magnitude of transition in black voting behavior which made the enormous deviation of 1966 possible, the city was partitioned among three groups of areas: those with less than 30 per cent nonwhite residents in 1960, those with between 30 and 69.9 per cent nonwhite, and those whose nonwhite population was 70 per cent or more (Table 6.5).

The black electorate's behavior in this decade is clearly the most arresting feature in this array. It has far less geographical variation—and presumably stratification variation as well—than does the white electorate. Of course, these black areas swang overwhelmingly toward Johnson in 1964; not only did they show a Republican defection ratio from 1960 of 77,[6] but the standard deviation was cut by more than half. Of even greater interest is the rotation of the black vote from 1964 to 1966, and again from 1966 to 1968, through virtually the entire range of possible Democratic support. It is known from surveys that blacks are among the most strongly party-identified members of the electorate, but Democratic party identification holds up no better for blacks confronted by a racist Democrat than it does for low-income whites in Cleveland or Gary who find that their party's candidate for mayor is black. This movement of Negro areas in Baltimore constitutes a brutal reminder that—as in the South of yesteryear and today—racial conflict in northern cities is quite capable of cutting through traditional party ties as easily as a knife through warm butter.

But what of the white electorate in Baltimore? There are a variety of methods of controlling for race as for other variables.

[6] For a definition of this measure, see Note 8 to Chapter III above.

Table 6.5 Variability in Voting Behavior: Baltimore, 1960–1968

	0–29.9% Nonwhite (Number = 48)		30–69.9% Nonwhite (Number = 13)	
	Mean %	Standard Deviation	Mean %	Standard Deviation
Democratic 1960	58.2	15.61	70.2	7.12
Democratic 1962	64.8	9.10	67.7	5.45
Democratic 1964	66.8	11.78	85.7	6.43
Democratic 1966	10.1	20.03	28.2	18.84
Republican 1966	35.8	19.84	58.4	18.42
Democratic 1968	49.2	17.12	77.8	11.79
Republican 1968	35.9	15.99	13.0	7.06
Wallace 1968	15.0	8.94	10.0	7.80
Nonwhite 1960	3.8	5.28	52.7	12.14

	70–100% Nonwhite (Number = 22)	
	Mean %	Standard Deviation
Democratic 1960	75.7	5.37
Democratic 1962	66.3	5.63
Democratic 1964	94.4	2.65
Democratic 1966	10.3	5.40
Republican 1966	78.1	6.13
Democratic 1968	90.2	5.01
Republican 1968	6.0	3.50
Wallace 1968	3.8	2.28
Nonwhite 1960	88.7	8.06

For the sake of simplicity, we shall examine, in Table 6.6, the correlation pattern within the forty-eight political areas where the white population in 1960 was 70 per cent or more of the total.

Over the past three presidential elections, there has been an extraordinary erosion of class polarization in the major-party

Table 6.6 Correlates of Voting Behavior,1960–1968: Baltimore's White Areas

1960 Census and Political Classification	% Democratic			
	1960	1962	1964	1966
% Democratic 1960	1.000	+.906	+.861	+.340
% Democratic 1962	+.906	1.000	+.693	+.586
% Democratic 1964	+.861	+.693	1.000	−.111
% Democratic 1966 (of 3-party vote)	+.340	+.586	−.111	1.000
% Democratic 1968	+.559	+.300	+.853	−.480
% Republican 1968	−.825	−.689	−.942	+.030
% Wallace 1968	+.420	+.670	+.057	+.884
% Foreign-Stock White	+.505	+.206	+.611	−.380
% Professional-Managerial	−.600	−.744	−.314	−.787
% Clerical-Sales	−.330	−.547	−.038	−.737
% Skilled and Semiskilled	+.485	+.658	+.182	+.806
% Unskilled and Service	+.464	+.564	+.285	+.500

1960 Census and Political Classification	% Dem. 1968	% Rep. 1968	% Wallace 1968
% Democratic 1960	+.559	−.825	+.420
% Democratic 1962	+.300	−.689	+.670
% Democratic 1964	+.853	−.942	+.057
% Democratic 1966 (of 3-party vote)	−.480	+.030	+.884
% Democratic 1968	1.000	−.858	−.375
% Republican 1968	−.858	1.000	−.153
% Wallace 1968	−.375	−.153	1.000
% Foreign-Stock White	+.650	−.468	−.394
% Professional-Managerial	+.001	+.433	−.790
% Clerical-Sales	+.262	+.122	−.740
% Skilled and Semiskilled	−.138	−.298	+.812
% Unskilled and Service	+.077	−.353	+.498

vote in these white areas. As the correlation between the proportion of professional-managerial people and the Democratic percentage declines—even shifting from the traditional negative to positive in 1968!—so a similar but inverse transformation can be seen in the relationship between working-class strength in the labor force and the Democratic vote. Once again this disappearance of Democratic class salience is not fully matched in the Republican vote; here too Wallace clearly drew a very large part of his vote from working-class areas with a traditional Democratic predominance. The Wallace vote, with its extreme class polarization, has a profile nearly identical with Mahoney's profile as the Democratic gubernatorial nominee of 1966.

What conclusions can be drawn from this data? In the first place, and of overriding electoral importance, is the effect of racial fears and antagonisms when they spill over into the arena of electoral politics. This polarization, in Baltimore and probably everywhere else, is most extreme as between the black population and blue-collar whites, particularly those who are somewhat above the bottom of the occupational pyramid. Traditional partisan and politically relevant group identifications provide little clue as to the patterns of electoral politics which arise under conditions of racial polarization. The Baltimore case makes it clear, however, that the appearance of similar candidates in such a context will lead to closely similar profiles of differential candidate appeal.

Second, both the strength and limitations of Wallace's penetration should be noted. The importance of George Wallace as a national political phenomenon is a measure of the rising tension, anxiety, and hatred which has developed during this decade as Negroes have gained significant legal protection and have moved into the core cities of our major metropolitan areas. As a semipopulist figure who has none of the disabilities in appealing to a mass electorate which were associated with

Goldwater's economic conservatism, he has been able to tap a major vein of "populist" support of both urban and rural variety. In doing so, he has eaten heavily into the structure of the pre-existing Democratic coalition. Yet it should be noted that while Wallace's strength was impressive in some areas of Delaware County and Baltimore, it remained a minority—a rather small minority, in fact—everywhere, particularly when compared with Mahoney's 1966 showing as a major-party candidate. There is some reason for supposing that, barring some unforeseen explosion, the appeal of a third-party candidate who capitalizes on racial fears will tend to be limited to those parts of the white urban electorate which are close to or on the front lines of America's social wars.

Third, the Baltimore data in particular suggest the possibility of a pro-Democratic realignment among middle- and upper-income groups as the economic cleavages of yesteryear become increasingly subordinated to other issues. The structure of the 1966 vote in Baltimore was an unusually dramatic, clear-cut case of an electoral alliance among middle- to upper-class whites, Jewish voters, and Negroes against whites of low-middle- to low-income and occupational status. The 1968 correlation profiles are, of course, much less dramatic. But they tend to support the thesis that a certain kind of realignment may be in the offing, one in which the Democratic Party may come to be increasingly the party of the technologically competent and technologically superfluous strata—the top and bottom of the paradigm suggested by Apter—while the Republican Party may become more and more explicitly the partisan vehicle for the defense of white "middle-America," the interests of the periphery against the center, and the values of the disintegrating Lockian-Horatio Alger creed which has dominated the country's political culture until very recently.

There is some reason to suppose, for example, that communities where college or university education is a dominant industry have undergone sharp realignment toward the Democrats during this decade. The evidence in Table 6.7 is not conclusive, perhaps, but it seems quite indicative. The sectional reorganization of electoral coalitions which is now going on presupposes, of course, that these communities—all but one of which is located in the Northeast—would reveal a plus Democratic trend relative to the nation as a whole. But when this is to some extent controlled by comparing the positioning of these communities with the Democratic percentages in their states, the upward Democratic trend seems almost as steep, except for the two New England state-university communities of Mansfield and Orono. The fact that all these communities except Swarthmore display such nearly identical partisan profiles in 1968 is also suggestive; and even in the case of Swarthmore—probably the most affluent of these six communities— the pro-Democratic realignment has been extremely steep.

No discussion of this incipient alignment pattern would be complete without at least a short review of one of its most spectacular and recent examples: the 1969 mayoralty election in New York City, in which the extent, strengths, and weaknesses of such a top-bottom coalition can be seen with exceptional clarity. The events of this campaign are well enough known to require no detailed discussion. John Lindsay's loss of the Republican primary, coupled with Mario Procaccino's capture of the Democratic nomination, created a context in which Lindsay was virtually compelled to construct a coalition of the rich and the poor against the white lower middle class. This coalition was able to triumph because—and perhaps only because—the intense opposition of New York's "great middle" to his re-election was divided between two candidates.

This election once again revealed the exceptional sophistication with which the urban black electorate is using its voting power these days, and the extent to which the traditional analytical canons of party identification as an anchor of voting

Table 6.7 Behavior of Communities with Academic Concentrations: Evidences of Realignment?

Community	Deviation	Deviation from National/State % Democratic *						% Dem. 1968	% Rep. 1968	% Wallace 1968
		1948	1952	1956	1960	1964	1968			
Mansfield, Conn.	National	−21.5	−11.0	−8.2	−4.4	+11.7	+13.8	56.5	40.4	3.1
	State	−18.3	−7.5	−2.3	−8.0	+5.1	+7.0			
Orono, Me.	National			−17.0	−5.2	+8.0	+13.5	56.2	43.2	0.6
	State			−3.8	+1.9	+0.5	+0.9			
Amherst, Mass.	National	−20.6	−18.9	−16.7	−10.4	+9.0	+14.7	57.6	40.5	2.0
	State	−25.7	−19.8	−15.0	−20.7	−6.2	−5.6			
Hanover, N.H.	National	−29.9	−19.0	−13.3	−11.6	+15.7	+11.4	54.1	45.0	0.9
	State	−26.6	−14.1	−5.0	−8.1	+13.1	+10.2			
Princeton, N.J.	National	−15.9	−4.4	−6.2	−3.0	+10.7	+15.2	57.9	39.0	3.2
	State	−11.2	−2.3	+1.4	−3.3	+6.0	+13.9			
Oberlin, Ohio	National	−27.8	−13.4	−12.4	−11.4	+6.9	+12.2	54.9	42.2	2.9
	State	−25.5	−12.0	−9.1	−8.0	+5.3	+12.0			
Swarthmore, Pa.	National	−40.7	−27.5	−25.2	−26.6	−10.5	−5.4	37.3	61.5	1.3
	State	−36.3	−29.9	−26.4	−27.7	−14.4	−10.3			

* Percentage Democratic of the total vote, 1948 and 1968; of the two-party vote, 1952–1964.

Table 6.8 Contemporary Electoral Movements in Black Areas and Puerto Rican Areas: The Case of New York City, 1966–1969 *

Year	Democratic	Republican	Other	Total
1966 Governor	82,833	47,226	21,014	151,073
1968 President	126,566	14,573	1,249	142,388
1969 Mayor	21,105	9,722	102,869 (Liberal)	133,696

Year	% Democratic	% Republican	% Other
1966 Governor	54.8	31.3	13.9
1968 President	88.9	10.2	0.9
1969 Mayor	15.8	7.3	76.9

* Seven assembly districts: 37, 54, 55, 70, 72, 74, and 78. It is hardly necessary to add that, with districts of such gross size, these particular ones selected are neither wholly black or Spanish-speaking nor do they contain anywhere near all of the voting members of these two groups in New York City.

behavior have lost their explanatory power. Unfortunately, the redrawing of assembly-district boundaries in the mid-1960's makes impossible a direct comparison of results for the same areas prior to 1966. Even so, the movement is sufficiently dramatic to merit presenting it in Table 6.8, both in absolute and relative terms. These shifts have produced a Q index of polarization between these seven assembly districts and the rest of the city which has ranged from +.279 in 1966 to +.678 in 1968 and —.627 in 1969.[7]

[7] This measure, Yule's Q, has been particularly widely used in legislative roll-call analysis. It is constructed from information, say, in a 2 x 2 table arrayed thus:

	Vote on Issue	
Voter	Yes	No
Category A	a	b
Category B	c	d

Lindsay's support by the bottom of New York's social structure was paralleled by an almost equally massive support
among both wealthy and not-so-wealthy but cosmopolitan
strata of the white population which are concentrated in Manhattan. The mean percentage for Lindsay of the three-candidate vote was 78.8 per cent in Harlem; in the three assembly
districts which cover the East Side of Manhattan from 14th
Street to about 97th Street, Lindsay's mean percentage of the
three-candidate vote was 69.8 per cent, compared with 41.8 per
cent for the city as a whole and 35.5 per cent for the four boroughs outside Manhattan.

Indeed, a kind of emergent "sectionalism" has been conspicuous in recent city elections. Like other kinds of sectionalism, it is the product of the emergence of profound cleavages at
the mass base which happen to be concentrated in geographical terms. Manhattan has increasingly become a borough without a white middle to lower middle class, where the wealthy
and the very poor, particularly black and Puerto Rican poor,
have become concentrated. It is also, of course, the citadel of
the political subculture of cosmopolitan liberalism both for the
nation and more particularly for the city itself. As the stresses
of metropolitan existence have mounted in steady progression,
the political animosity between the four outer boroughs—

and is computed according to the formula $Q = \dfrac{ad - bc}{ad + bc}$. For a discussion
of this and similar measures of association, see Lee F. Anderson *et al.*,
Legislative Roll-Call Analysis (Evanston, Ill.: Northwestern University
Press, 1966), pp. 50–51. It has rather infrequently been employed in
American studies of mass voting behavior, at least partly because aggregate statistics do not yield a sufficiently large polarization profile under
normal conditions to make it particularly useful. Under the conditions
which have emerged in the past decade, however, the case is entirely
different. Thus, Q related to the percentages Democratic and Republican
and black and white in geographical areas of Cleveland is approximately
+.98 for both the 1967 and 1969 mayoral elections. Such electoral polarizations have been almost unknown in American politics at any large aggregate level. One of the chief characteristics of the 1960's is that they
have become commonplace.

where Procaccino actually won a plurality of the vote—and the cosmopolis of Manhattan has become steadily more acute.

New York's 1969 mayoral election brought this fracture into clear relief. Here we can examine Q polarizations over the period from 1936 through 1969, and the emergent cleavage

Table 6.9 Polarization Between Manhattan and the Rest of New York City: Q Scores, 1936–1969

Year	Office	Q
1936	President	−.021
1937	Mayor	+.056
1940	President	+.023
1941	Mayor	−.097
1944	President	+.131
1945	Mayor	−.024
1948	President	+.056
1949	Mayor	−.033
1950	Mayor	+.049
1952	President	+.116
1953	Mayor	+.022
1954	Governor	+.056
1956	President	+.120
1957	Mayor	+.055
1958	Governor	+.037
1960	President	+.076
1961	Mayor (2-candidates)	+.020
1961	Mayor (3 candidates)	+.096
1962	Governor	+.013
1964	President	+.259
1965	Mayor	−.199
1966	Governor	−.180
1968	President	+.256
1969	Mayor (2 candidates)	−.553
1969	Mayor (3 candidates)	−.564

pattern of the past five years is evident. Of particular interest
in Table 6.9 is the stability of the series from 1952 through
1962. Of course, the slight positive Q suggests two points:
Manhattan, with fewer middle-class residential areas, was
somewhat more Democratic than the white residential boroughs as a whole, but the difference was both extremely small
and quite stable. From the 1964 election, the pattern changes
abruptly; in presidential elections, the Q measure is more than
twice as large as it was previously. Moreover, the relationship

Table 6.10   Correlations, Means, and Standard Deviations:
The New York Picture, 1969

Correlation Pair	r	r² × 100
Lindsay 1969/Democratic 1968	+.802	64.32
Marchi 1969/Republican 1968	+.859	73.72
Procaccino 1969/Democratic 1968	−.344	11.80

1969 Mayoral Candidate	Mean	Variance	Standard Deviation
Lindsay (Liberal-Independent)	44.5	348.46	18.67
Marchi (Republican-Conservative)	21.4	148.34	12.18
Procaccino (Democratic)	34.1	158.69	12.60

becomes unstable—positive in presidential elections, negative
in state and local elections. Finally, there is a gigantic leap
forward in this measure of borough polarization in 1969 associated with the smashing of pre-existing party alignments in
the city, particularly in Manhattan, and with the full emergence
of the successful Lindsay top-bottom coalition.

Finally, the shape of the new coalitions can be grasped
through correlation analysis. In Table 6.10, correlation of the
distribution of the vote for the three candidates in the city's
sixty-eight assembly districts with the 1968 results makes clear,

among other things, both the desperate position of the Democratic Party and the extreme degree to which Lindsay has become isolated from the Republican mass base.

The variances and standard deviations provide an alternative means of measuring the chief feature of this election: the distribution of the Lindsay vote was far more dispersed than that of either of the other two candidates. This corresponds both to the U-shaped distribution of support for Lindsay as one moves from the top to the middle and then to the bottom of the socioeconomic structure of the city, and also to the division of the anti-Lindsay vote. This division was especially disastrous to Procaccino's chances for victory in middle-class areas in Queens, for example, where the continuing hold of Republican party identification and support led to a typical pattern in which Procaccino and Marchi ran neck and neck, with Lindsay trailing far behind.

While this seems dramatic evidence that the Apterite paradigm of postindustrial social stratification has considerable relevance to today's politics, it would be premature, to say the least, to conclude that a top-bottom alliance against the "great middle" is either large enough or stable enough to produce the basis for a majority coalition in any sixth party system which may emerge. Several aspects of contemporary electoral politics—indeed of the 1969 elections generally—stand in the way of easy acceptance of such a view, even though decades hence we might find such a coalition to be the majority basis for a seventh party system. In the first place, as has been reiterated time and again by analysts of American politics, New York is not the nation: in this respect, William Cahill's extraordinarily uniformly distributed landslide in the gubernatorial race across the Hudson River in New Jersey—a state of suburbs—may be more instructive for national perspectives than the mayoral contest in New York City.

Second, while New York is not the nation, its immense social and political problems can be viewed as those which will emerge in more and more acute form throughout the country. In this context, the fragility of the Lindsay coalition should be remembered. He won, and winning counts in politics; but he ran 7 per cent behind the poll estimates and his final tally of 41.8 per cent—a margin of only 6.8 per cent over Procaccino—reveals what is, even in New York City, a minority coalition at best.

Despite the outcome, "urban populism" remains very much alive and well in the citadel of cosmopolitan liberalism. A fusion between it and the respectable conservatism of the better-off strata of America's "great middle" might well prove unstoppable even in New York City, not to mention the nation. The nature of Mayor Lindsay's coalition is such that he may be well advised to affiliate himself with the Democrats, either formally or informally. The structure of recent American political behavior, however, makes it very clear that of the two major parties, the Democratic Party is in much the more serious trouble. Its capacity to retain its hold over enough of even its nonsouthern coalitional elements to remain ascendant in American politics is very much in doubt. The long-range prospects that a top-bottom coalition could construct enough heterogeneous appeal to win national elections are probably good, since both appear to be growing at the expense of the middle. The short- and intermediate-range prospects, however, are an entirely different matter.

Finally, the transitional character of the last two presidential elections can be studied by turning to analysis at the macro level. Both Gerald Pomper and the present author have recently argued that one measure of critical realignment, viewed over the past century and more, is the existence of systematic disturbance in the very high autocorrelations which are usually derived when partisan percentages in one election are correlated by state with those of the immediately preceding and

succeeding ones.[8] The "normal" range of these autocorrelations
is between +.90 and +1.00, a way of quantifying the obvious
point that in stable phases of the electoral cycle the relationship of the component parts of the voting system to each other
tends to be extremely stable. In realigning elections, however,
a significant decline in r occurs—in the last two realignments,
to below +.80. The review of these correlations since 1940 in
Table 6.11 might lead one to overstate the immensity of the
political transitions over the past generation, since the analysis
is at a very gross level; nevertheless, it already represents the
quantitatively greatest transition in the entire span of this
series.

Several points clearly arise from this array. There is a sys-

Table 6.11 Continuity and Change: Correlations by
State, 1940–1968

Election Pair	$r =$	$r^2 \times 100 =$
1940 Democratic–1944 Democratic	+.98	96.04
1944 Democratic–1948 Democratic	+.96	92.16
1948 Democratic–1952 Democratic	+.74	54.76
1952 Democratic–1956 Democratic	+.60	36.00
1956 Democratic–1960 Democratic	+.54	29.16
1960 Democratic–1964 Democratic	−.11	1.21
1964 Democratic–1968 Democratic (3-party)	+.86	73.96
1960 Democratic–1968 Democratic (3-party)	+.30	9.00
1964 Democratic–1968 Democratic (2-party)	+.23	5.29
1960 Democratic–1968 Democratic (2-party)	+.72	51.84
1960 Democratic–1968 Wallace	+.12	1.44
1964 Democratic–1968 Wallace	−.80	64.00
1968 Democratic–1968 Wallace	−.76	57.76
1968 Republican–1968 Wallace	−.60	36.00

[8] Cf. Walter Dean Burnham, "American Voting Behavior and the 1964
Election," *op. cit.;* and Gerald M. Pomper, *Elections in America* (New
York: Dodd, Mead, 1969), pp. 99–125, 268–69.

tematic downward progression in the size of the correlations from 1948, which finally yields a faintly *negative* but above all virtually random relationship for the 1960–64 pair; this, of course, has much to do (particularly in 1964) with the contemporary revolution in southern politics. The transitional nature of 1964 is clearly suggested by the very high +.86 relationship between the Democratic vote in 1964 and the Democratic share of the three-party vote in 1968; yet when the Wallace vote is factored out, the relationship drops precipitately, while that existing between 1960 Democratic and 1968 Democratic rises from +.30 in a three-party context to +.72 when the major-party vote is considered. Finally, the Wallace correlations reveal, as one might expect, a weak positive relationship with the 1960 Democratic vote and a significantly greater negative relationship with both the 1964 and 1968 Democratic percentages than with the 1968 Republican percentage.

The profoundly transitional nature of the 1960's seems to be captured admirably by these figures; so does the ambiguity of the transition. A major regionally structured transformation in the bases of electoral support lurks just below the surface of these correlations: the Democratic share of the southern vote has declined catastrophically in the past decade, while the extreme northern and northeastern states have undergone both a relative and absolute Democratic shift in presidential elections.

In attempting to evaluate the possibility that all this movement constitutes in a classical sense a critical realignment in its first stages, certain basic properties of past critical realignments in this country should be recalled. They have been constituent acts, yes; they have brought about redefinitions reaching to the fundamentals of our political economy, yes. But they have been bought at a very high price. They have arisen only under conditions of the greatest dislocations in economy and society. They have strongly tended to move the focus of our electoral politics from procedure to substance, from tradition or candidate charm to issues, but the polarizations in every case have placed enormous strains on consensus. Without exception such critical realignments have had visible civil-war potential, a potential which in one famous case was actually realized.

What happens during critical realignment seems to be nothing less than an intense, if temporary and partial, revolutionizing of a middle class whose normal involvement in electoral politics is traditionalist or passive-participant. The strains on American political consensus which are always associated with such exceptional events rather clearly reveal, moreover, that that consensus is far more procedural and political than substantive or social.

The potential fracture lines around which a sixth party system would be organized are, unlike those of the New Deal realignment but very much like those of all preceding ones, overwhelmingly horizontal: black against white, peripheral regions against the center, "parochials" against "cosmopolitans," blue-collar whites against both blacks and affluent liberals, the American "great middle," with its strong attachment to the values of the traditional American political formula, against urban cosmopolitans, intellectuals, and students who have largely left that old credo behind. The mixture has become explosive enough, even leaving aside the accelerating effects of the endless Vietnam imbroglio, to be ignited by some sharp crisis. What would happen should it be ignited would, in detail, be anyone's guess, depending upon the specific context and the availability of effective political entrepreneurs who knew how to capitalize on their opportunity.

One alternative might be a continuing Republican effort to absorb the Wallace following, and with it its militarism and racism, coupled with a Democratic pursuit of a top-bottom alliance, external disengagement, and increased welfarism. Another might be the continued growth of a third-party movement and its increasing penetration of the lower and lower-middle strata of the white population until it reached perhaps a quarter or more of the total electorate. Whatever the specific configuration, a political realignment organized around these terms would have as large a civil-war potential, would place as great a strain on political consensus—including, perhaps, the willingness of the losers in the electoral-politics arena to accept the outcome of an election—as any critical realignment in our history. A sixth party system organized in such terms, and with the issues which would have to be bound up with its organization, would have the most sinister overtones, for its agenda would probably entail nothing less than either the speedy liquidation of those aspects of the traditional American political formula which have stood in the way of central planning for change or—and perhaps more probably—a last-ditch effort to reimpose that formula's dominant position in the political culture by force if necessary.

But there are two things which stand, so far at least, in the way of an easy acceptance of such an outcome. The first is the gross decomposition of the hold of party on the electorate which has already been discussed at length. The second is the absence, thus far, of a crystallizing factor. If historical parallels have any contemporary relevance, the mere existence of explosive volatility in the electorate or of accumulating strain in the socioeconomic system is not enough by itself to produce critical realignment in the classical sense. For this a detonator is needed, some triggering event of scope and brutal force great enough to produce the mobilizations required from a normally passive-participant middle-class electorate. The dominant public-policy purpose which has underlain federal economic policy since the 1930's has been to prevent economic collapse from ever recurring—a choice which is informed at

least as much by concern over the destabilizing *political* consequences of such recurrence as by any economic or human
considerations.

It has been characteristic of these great convulsions known
as critical realignments that the disasters triggering them must
not only be profound but must be in the nature of sharp, sudden blows, and recurrent collapses of an unregulated market
economy have, historically, been among the most important.
Such blows must be hard enough to open up a relatively sudden gap between expectations and perceived political, social,
and economic realities. They must also hit enough sectors of
society more or less simultaneously to produce the masses of
abnormally politicized voters needed for critical realignment
to occur. And the context of disaster must have sufficiently
clear political focus and relevance that the ensuing mobilization's major goal is to capture the apparatus of state, at least
for the time being.

The foregoing discussion has emphasized that the present
condition of American societal development contains a number
of what Marxists call "internal contradictions," some of which
clearly have issue clusters around which a critical realignment
could well be structured. But the detonator has not yet appeared on the scene. There have, of course, been ghetto and
student riots with subsequent backlash responses from the
largely middle-class, white, and middle-aged electorate. Yet
thus far these upheavals seem too narrowly defined socially,
or in terms of their *direct* impact upon the lives of the "great
middle," to produce countermobilization as a defensive bloc
against pressure from the top and bottom of the political system.

Similarly, among the most important agencies of political
dislocation at the present time are the Vietnam war and the
accumulating social disasters in our metropolitan areas. However, so far the war has cut across traditional party lines. It

involves an area of policy—that of foreign and military affairs
—in which mass public opinion is notoriously less focused and
anchored than in the domestic issues which form the stuff of
our electoral politics, and in any case has involved a rather
gradual buildup followed by an even more gradual scaling
down. The war has had a profound impact on the political
system: it has been a significant accelerator of domestic group
tension and seems to have contributed to the erosion of the
Lockian political culture's hold on the beliefs of many Americans. Yet in the last analysis its political impact has—so far,
at least—been so ambiguous as to raise doubts that it will
move from being an accelerator of tensions to being a cat-
alyst of realignment. The war has been incrementalized to
the point that, if it be a disaster, it is one to which the American voter may be able to adjust.

It is also not difficult to find evidence of accumulating social
disaster in our metropolitan areas. But this is a gradual and
cumulative phenomenon, not a sudden and dramatic one. We
went to war with Japan in 1941 over an attack that was far less
devastating in scope and intensity than the destruction to be
found in almost any large American city today. But the destruction came unexpectedly, as a sharp blow, from a foreign
power. The present urban deterioration has matured as a result of our own internal social and political processes, and it
has been unfolding gradually for decades. So far, we have
somehow learned to live with and adapt to it. There is plenty
of evidence of countermobilization by trapped lower-class
whites in local contests involving racial antagonisms. But as
long as most of the "great middle" can exercise their Lockian
prerogative of evading the confrontation by flight into remote
suburban reaches there is little reason to suppose that they will
feel under enough pressure to realign toward a repressive "urban populism." The amount of electoral disaggregation which
is now abundantly visible at every level of electoral politics

tends to reveal the immense difficulty of organizing cohesive majorities around such issues on a metropolitanwide, much less nationwide, basis; and that disaggregation itself, as has been emphasized here, has placed great barriers in the way of creating such a majority. It seems unlikely that, in the absence of a sudden increase in the rate of deterioration or in the intensity and scope of America's social wars, the plight of the city could provide the motive force for critical realignment.

Certainly, one may hope that if such preconditions as have been described here are necessary for critical realignment to recur, we will be spared a future example, for two reasons. First, no humane observer would *prefer,* surely, to see a sudden steep increase in mass misery, anxiety, or alienation in the United States, even if he perceived it as the only possible setting in which the social change he thought desirable might take place. Second, even if one were indifferent to this consideration, it is probable that any force great enough to produce "classical" critical realignment under present conditions would also be great enough to break the system altogether, with consequences of incalculable magnitude.

On the other hand, as we have suggested, the party system may have already moved beyond the possibility of critical realignment because of the dissolution of party-related identification and voting choice at the mass base. Such a development would in itself mark one of the great turning points in the history of American politics. Political parties have had a profoundly significant constituent function in our political system. This function has been most characteristically realized through critical realignments with durable consequences. The disappearance of these parties as the primary channel through which mass opinion is articulated would necessarily imply, therefore, a most profound and irreversible transformation in the American constitution itself. It is not easy to construct any precise estimate of what American electoral politics without widespread party identification and party voting would look like. We may suppose, however, that political decision-makers would have wider discretion, particularly in foreign and military issue areas, than they have even now, and that specific interest groups would enjoy even more influence on policy-making than they do now. To the extent that the erosion of party at the mass base is joined with mobilization for self-defense within the American "great middle"—as may very well happen—we would probably find that the political system had attempted to take for its motto the last sentence of the preface to *1066 and All That:* "History is at an end; this History is therefore final." [9] One may doubt whether this outcome would be preferable, after all, to the alternative of critical realignment; for it would certainly have terminated the historical role in reshaping our institutions and our political system which has been played by the American electorate from time to time.

[9] W. C. Sellar and R. J. Yeatman, *1066 and All That* (New York: E. P. Dutton, 1931), p. viii.

7

Critical Elections and the Dynamics of American Politics

The data in this study have revealed the existence of two dominant patterns in American electoral politics: the existence of critical realignments which have many behavioral features in common separating them from normal election sequences and which, moreover, periodically recur; and the post-1900 trend toward decomposition of political parties as action instrumentalities. What light do these processes shed upon the peculiarities of the American political system? In particular, how might they relate to the extraordinary hold of a single master set of political values on Americans?

One may begin, so far as critical realignments are concerned, with a paradox noted by Louis Hartz: the effective working of the pluralized governmental structures established by the framers of the Constitution has been dependent upon the failure of the social-conflict model which many of them accepted to be relevant to American conditions.[1] Such dispersed structures can function because, and very probably only because, the Americans who work them share the same broad set of sociopolitical values and because such values have never hitherto been effectively challenged, much less overthrown, by any politically significant group. The reasons for this exceptional state of affairs have been explored at length by American cultural historians and others, and need not detain us here. The point is that the overwhelming majority of Americans have accepted bourgeois individualism and its Lockian-liberal political variant as their consensual value system.

In operational terms this has meant the construction of a political system which is—in domestic matters, at any rate—dispersive and fragmented; a political system which is dedicated to the defeat, except temporarily and under the direct pressure of overwhelming crisis, of any attempt to generate domestic sovereignty; a political system whose chief function has been the maintenance of a high wall of separation between political conflict on one side and the socioeconomic system on the other. A deep-seated dialectic has operated over the entire history of the country: while the socioeconomic system has developed and transformed itself from the beginning with an energy and thrust unparalleled in modern history, the political system from parties to policy institutions has remained astonishingly little transformed in its characteristics and methods of operation.

Samuel P. Huntington has recently advanced the view that the American political system is, in effect, a "Tudor polity." It is studded with functioning survivals of such early-modern political phenomena as an assumed *consensus rei publicae*, the persistence of a considerable diffusion of governmental structures

[1] Louis Hartz, *The Liberal Tradition in America* (New York: Harcourt, Brace, 1955), pp. 85–86.

and thus a relative lack of governmental rationalization, and above all by the failure of anything comparable to the internal sovereignty found in other Western societies to develop here.[2] Nor are these survivals vestigial, vermiform appendices of the American body politic; they dominate, in fact they define, the American political system. This system is patently the most archaic of any in existence in a modern industrial society. It functions and survives essentially because no very large group within the society is normally motivated to organize for the capture of state power in order to inaugurate central control over and transformations of the socioeconomic system. This lack of motivation in turn arises from the reception of Lockian individualism, its dissemination in one variant or another through the vast majority of the population, and, consequently, the virtual unthinkability of such a project for collective action.

The political parties are and normally always have been organizationally preoccupied with winning elections and with managing the tensions between the subcoalitional groups of which they are composed. The secret of their stability, their overwhelming dominance over the electoral-politics system, and their lack of capacity for or concern with detailed policy control when returned with "majorities" to elective offices lies in this overriding reality. Cohesive majorities normally do not exist at the electoral level any more than in legislative bodies. But above all there is no firm foundation in any but the most marginal members of the parties' mass coalitions for their conversion into instrumentalities of *collective* purposes and action. On the contrary, the increasingly fine division of labor in this society has, along with affluence, suburbanization, and other factors, produced a stepwise adjustment of our electoral politics to industrialism: the erosion of party as an action intermediary and the conversion of elections into candidate-

[2] Samuel P. Huntington, *Political Order in Changing Societies* (New Haven: Yale University Press, 1968), pp. 93–139.

image affairs for which only the very wealthy or those close to the very wealthy need apply. One is inclined to speculate that, as long as economic growth is not seriously undercut by depression, the survival of middle-class individualist political values and the continuing role of such factors as those mentioned above will serve only to reinforce the bluntness of the party as an instrument for the pursuit of broad political goals.

Huntington has also advanced the thesis that the American political pattern constitutes one of three "patterns of modernization." [3] But does not the survival of this "Tudor polity" in so nearly unchanged a form demonstrate the opposite, that political modernization is precisely what is most foreign to the American political experience? Political modernization has been conspicuous by its absence here, assuming that such a concept presupposes systematic transformation toward, for example, greater rationalization of governmental structures and processes. What have been the preconditions for its emergence elsewhere in the Western world? First, a pre-existing *consensus rei publicae,* if one exists, must be terminated as the members of antagonistic collectivities within the society become politically self-conscious. Second, the pre-existing socioeconomic structure must have sufficient prescriptive rigidity and diversity of life-styles and values within it to block modernizing change through its own autonomous processes. This would presuppose that, if such change is to be brought about, a cohesive, identifiable *sovereign* power center in the apparatus of state must emerge and be used by those in charge of it in order to bring about desired change in the socioeconomic system over the resistance of those with vested material or ideological interests in the existing order. Third, politics at some point must come generally to be regarded as a struggle for the capture or defense of this center, with the aim of using state power as a positive means of bringing about substantive

[3] *Ibid.,* pp. 93–98.

transformations in the socioeconomic system or, alternatively, of preventing them.

But it is precisely these preconditions which both the institutional structure and the political culture have worked persistently to prevent, and almost always with success. Only once in American history did antagonisms over social fundamentals burst through this elaborate Lockian defense network. It is suggestive of the limits of American politics in their "normal" state that the consequences were truly revolutionary, and that they involved *both* civil war and a temporary if effective assertion of internal sovereignty quite at variance with the American political tradition.

But the Civil War is the rare if instructive exception. If material and cultural circumstances are favorable to rapid socioeconomic development as a quasiautonomous process—and the testimony of acute observers from Tocqueville to Hartz is overwhelming that they have been in the United States—there is no apparent reason why profound transformations of the political system in such a society should *ever* occur. If one can imagine an electoral process in which political parties have gradually ceased to have much operational importance, one can for the same reasons imagine a political regime whose survival depends upon the negation of "political development" if the latter requires the creation of internal sovereignty and collective struggle for control of the apparatus of state.[4]

[4] One very curious datum indeed arises from this study which does not seem to square at all with Huntington's discussion of America: the material on trends in electoral participation. (*Ibid.*, pp. 122–33.) He asks, for example, "Why did the early and rapid expansion of political participation fail to breed violence and instability in the United States?" (p. 128.) The answer to this is that it *did* breed it: development of mass communication and of the mobilization of the adult male electorate into large party formations of nationwide scope helped to bring about mass consciousness of the acute antebellum discrepancy in labor systems and social values which existed in the United States. It thus made possible a civil war in 1861 which was not possible in 1821. See Walter Dean Burnham, "Party Systems and the Political Process," in Chambers and Burn-

The Lockian cultural monolith, however, is based upon a social assumption which comes repeatedly into collision with reality. The assumption, of course, is not only that the autonomy of socioeconomic life from political direction is the prescribed fundamental law for the United States, but that this autonomous socioeconomic development will proceed with enough smoothness, uniformity, and general benefits to individuals that it will be entirely compatible with the usual functioning of Lockian political structures. Yet the high (though far from impermeable) wall of separation between politics and society which emerges as a result is periodically threatened with inundations from the American social world outside. The reason is clear enough. Autonomous socioeconomic development, emphasizing something approximating the outer limits of individual freedom possible in an organized society, has been a possible and even relatively successful way of allocating scarce resources in the United States. But it has not been smooth, uniform, or always generally beneficial in its operations and consequences. The recurring social or economic maladjustments have been so large that the normal processes of American politics no longer suffice to contain their

ham, *op. cit.*, p. 283. Leaving this enormous lapse into violence and instability aside, American corporate elites toward the end of the last century gave every evidence of believing that full participation and the existing very high level of partisan mobilization of the lower orders might lead to "anarchy" and "revolution." They acted accordingly.

If there were "discontinuities" in the expansion of political participation in Europe, there were also "discontinuities" in the United States, but in the direction of *shrinkage* in this participation. Of course, they tended to be more diffuse here than there, as was to be expected. But they were sufficiently sharp and "European" in the southern states at any rate. Once socioeconomic modernization had reached a certain point in the United States, the requirements of corporate capitalism and of political democracy came into increasing, if largely unacknowledged, conflict. Democracy was at least the partial loser in this struggle—a very different view of the American record from that suggested by Huntington. Perhaps some agreement could be found in the proposition that this was, after all, possible in the United States only because of the dominance of the factors which both Hartz and Huntington emphasize.

political effects.

The periodic rhythm of American electoral politics, the cycle of oscillation between the normal and the disruptive, corresponds precisely to the existence of largely unfettered developmental change in the socioeconomic system and its absence in the country's political institutions. Indeed, it is a prime quantitative measure of the interaction between the two. The socioeconomic system develops but the institutions of electoral politics and policy formation remain essentially unchanged. Moreover, they do not have much capacity to adjust incrementally to demand arising from socioeconomic dislocations. Dysfunctions centrally related to this process become more and more visible, until finally entire classes, regions, or other major sectors of the population are directly injured or come to see themselves as threatened by imminent danger. Then the triggering event occurs, critical realignments follow, and the universe of policy and of electoral coalitions is broadly redefined. It is at such moments that the constitution-making role of the American voter becomes most visible, and his behavior, one suspects, least resembles the normal pattern described in survey research work done during the Eisenhower era.

In this context, then, critical realignment emerges as decisively important in the study of the dynamics of American politics. It is as symptomatic of political nonevolution in this country as are the archaic and increasingly rudimentary structures of the political parties themselves. But even more importantly, critical realignment may well be defined as the chief tension-management device available to so peculiar a political system. Historically it has been the chief means through which an underdeveloped political system can be recurrently brought once again into some balanced relationship with the changing socioeconomic system, permitting a restabilization of our politics and a redefinition of the dominant Lockian political formula in terms which gain overwhelming support from the current generation. Granted the relative inability of our political institutions to make gradual adjustments along vectors of *emergent* political demand, critical realignments have been as inevitable as they have been necessary to the normal workings of American politics. Thus once again there is a paradox: the conditions which decree that coalitional negotiation, bargaining, and incremental, unplanned, and gradual policy change become the dominant characteristic of American politics in its normal state also decree that it give way to abrupt, disruptive change with considerable potential for violence. So central has this dialectic been to the workings of our "Tudor polity" across time that the disappearance of one of its key elements, the critical realignment, could only mean that the most fundamental turning point in the entire history of this political system has occurred.

Such a dynamically oriented frame of reference presupposes a holistic view of American politics which is radically different from that which until very recently has tended to dominate the professional literature. The models of American political life and political processes with which we are most familiar emphasize the well-known attributes of pluralist democracy. There are not stable policy majorities. Intense and focused minorities with well-defined interests exert influence on legislation and administrative rule making out of all proportion to their size. The process involves gradual, incremental change secured after bargaining has been completed among a wide array of interested groups who are prepared to accept the conditions of bargaining. It is true that such descriptions apply to a "politics as usual" which is an important fragment of political reality in the United States, but to describe this fragment as the whole of that reality is to assume an essentially ideological posture whose credibility can be maintained only by ignoring the complementary dynamics of American politics as a whole. The study of the electoral process and its relationship to the effectiveness of the system's integration of the demands made of it and to the political elites chosen through it provides an important key for a broader understanding.

The reality of this process taken as a whole seems quite different from the pluralist vision. It is one shot through with escalating tensions, periodic electoral upheavals, and repeated redefinitions of the rules and outcomes-in-general of the political game, as well as redefinitions—by no means always broadening ones—of those who are in fact permitted to play it. One very basic characteristic of American party politics which emerges from a contemplation of critical realignments is a profound incapacity of established political leadership to adapt itself sequentially—or even incrementally?—to emergent political demand generated by the losers in our stormy socioeconomic transformations. American political parties are not action instrumentalities of definable and broad social collectivities; as organizations they are, consequently, interested in control of offices but not of government in the broader sense of which we have been speaking. It follows from this that once successful routines are established or reestablished for winning office, there is no motivation among party leaders to disturb the routines of the game. These routines are disturbed not by adaptive change within the party-policy system, but by the application of overwhelming external force.

One major implication of the foregoing discussion is that a mode of analysis which focuses on these dynamics may permit us to recombine and establish connections in new and conceptually fruitful ways between events and transformations which are already well known. Assuming its validity, it should also lead knowledgeable students of American politics to develop hypotheses whose testing will result in the discovery of phenomena which have hitherto been only rudimentarily explored in the professional literature.

An example of the former is the very sharp transition around

1890–1900 in the mean tenure of Speakers of the House at the time of their first election as presiding officer, discussed earlier. Of course, this quantum change had nothing directly to do with the mass voting behavior with which we have been primarily concerned. It is, rather, part of the process of "institutionalization of the House of Representatives" described in two recent articles by Nelson Polsby and his associates. But Polsby's data, particularly in his second article, make clear that there were decisive cutting points in the larger development of institutionalization which can also be pinpointed as occurring at the same time. If one then considers the enormous changes in the bases of support for the parties which occurred during the 1894–96 realignment in the arena of mass politics, another part of the puzzle falls into place.

Turning further to the changes in the Supreme Court's policies and institutional role in the political system during this period, an entirely new dimension comes into view. These changes were quite nonincremental and of the most far-reaching importance for the workings of public policy over the next forty years. In the space of a few years, the basic structure of juridical defense of industrial and other elites from mass pressure was brought into being, and for the next generation—until, indeed, the results of the next critical realignment made its position untenable—the Supreme Court embarked on its "quest for judicial supremacy" over public economic-allocation policy.[5]

By the time one has completed the task of assembling and synchronizing such fragments, he is confronted with the picture of a dynamic system whose parts are interacting to pro-

---

[5] The literature on this subject is enormous. One classic exposition by an active participant in its liquidation is Robert H. Jackson, *The Quest for Judicial Supremacy*. (New York: Alfred A. Knopf, 1941). A seminal study of its legal-cultural origins remains Benjamin Twiss, *Lawyers and the Constitution*. (Princeton: Princeton University Press, 1942). The need to integrate this subject into a larger theory of American policy dynamics is obvious.

duce a revised structure of policy and of institutional relationships. This structure is systematically patterned, is specific to the particular political era in which it occurs and which it dominates, and has obvious functional utility in fulfilling dominant system and elite needs.

In this context, the point should be emphasized that the periodization of American political history which emerges into clear view from an examination of these dynamics is of importance not only to historians but to students of contemporary American political processes. Nowhere is the significance of the life-history of political phenomena more important than in a nation where political modernization has been conspicuous by its absence. More concretely, it can be demonstrated that during the fourth party system of 1896–1932 many basic changes in the political system emerged which were functionally related to each other, and that a number of these developed trends toward completeness which were reversed only temporarily or not at all after that system was replaced by its successor. Among these the institutionalization of the House of Representatives and the increasing dissociation between presidential and congressional election results are among the most important.

What does it mean that such important elements of an essentially reactionary structure of politics should have survived after the demise of its other elements, and indeed should be flourishing in our own time? Some preliminary answers to this question have been given here. But the question itself, in one phrasing or another, cannot be asked at all unless the analyst is aware of these periodic transformations both generally and in some concrete detail; and, in whatever form it is asked, it is a question of very great importance.

The behavioral dynamics of American electoral politics broadly correspond, then, to the needs and expectations of a people which is socially heterogeneous but is overwhelmingly committed to an individualist, middle-class, and achievement-oriented social value system. Several concluding hypotheses and observations can be derived from this cardinal reality. In the first place, the decay of the political party as action intermediary, which has a trend line some seventy years long, can easily be perceived as part of a larger mechanism by which the political system has preserved its stability under the enormous transforming impact of industrial development and the urbanization of the country's population. This response of the system as a whole, as Theodore J. Lowi has pointed out, has been overwhelmingly in the direction of political disaggregation, at least in the arenas of domestic politics.[6] A tremendously pluralized structure of policy articulation has matured in the contemporary welfare/warfare-state era of American politics. This can quite appropriately be regarded as a stable-dominant form of American politics in an era where some central regulation of the economic system has become necessary for minimal political stability, but also where the traditional middle-class individualist ideology, as modified somewhat by this constraint, has continued to dominate the political culture.

Functional collectivism is an integral part of industrialization and urbanization in the modern world, in the United States no less than elsewhere. But it seems evident that the creation of political movements and structures which reflect this fact in operational terms cannot transcend the limits of group consciousness or extreme pluralism in decisional structures without a basic transformation in the American political system. In the last analysis, this system can absorb groupism, accompanied by its colorful array of subcoalitional combat in electoral politics and the proliferation of the pressure system, because groupism *does not raise the issue of domestic sovereignty*. It permits the continuation under high-industrial-

[6] Theodore J. Lowi, *The End of Liberalism* (New York: W. W. Norton, 1969).

ism conditions of a very large private-sector role in shaping authoritative allocations of resources. In a great many respects, the Lockian individualist dogma can be applied as easily to the individual group, or the individual-as-member-of-group, as to the atomic human being of classical theory. But this individualist dispensation probably cannot assimilate very much larger social solidarities without changing into something substantively different from what it was.

We have sketched in some detail the erosion of pre-existing party structures and linkages which can be traced back to the 1890–1900 decade. This grew out of the incapacity of the earlier parties to adapt their structures, mass coalitions, and political goals in a way which corresponded with the rise of functional collectivism in society and economy. And this, in turn, was merely the behavioral certification of the failure of any broadly based collectivist political consciousness to emerge, then or later, among Americans. It was not possible in the last analysis for democratic consciousness and democratic mass organizational structures to transcend the postulates or the limitations of middle-class individualist democracy. Thus, when the conflict between industrial capitalism and the pre-existing democratic structure came into the open, it was in the first place not very widely perceived as a conflict at all, except among certain marginal intellectual and labor groups; and it eventuated in the displacement of democracy, not of industrial capitalism.

The price which has been paid in our public life for the survival of the Lockian political dispensation into an era of big organization and high industrialism has been very high. Scholars and political activists have only recently turned to the exploration of some of these costs. But until now the vast majority of Americans have been prepared to accept them because they have corresponded to the survival of their most basic sociopolitical values. But the full effects of the immense population transfers of the past generation are becoming felt; urbanization continues; and the population of the country is now well past the 200 million mark. There is an increasingly obvious conflict between the political values of the middle strata and the emergent need to employ central allocative and public authority to direct the future course of socioeconomic transformation.

The pre-existing welfarist allocation system, as Lowi has pointed out, was a system far more preoccupied with solving ad hoc problems than with maintaining justice. Not until the 1960's did this emerge as a central ingredient in the current transitional crisis. But there are certain kinds of values which disaggregated welfarism cannot allocate without undermining its own legitimacy, and there are a wide range of emergent allocation problems which cannot be effectively reached by it at all. Whether one accepts or rejects Daniel P. Moynihan's analysis of the failures of the Great Society, it seems hard to deny that this massive effort to deal with contemporary conflict in New Dealish terms has been a failure, that if anything it has exacerbated the conflicts it was designed to resolve, and that it has served to undermine the very legitimacy of our thoroughly Lockian institutions of representation and resource allocation.[7]

The evidence points overwhelmingly to the conclusion that the American polity has entered the most profound turning point in its history. The task confronting it now may be no less than the construction of instrumentalities of domestic sovereignty to limit individual freedom in the name of collective necessity, as Lowi implicitly argues.[8] If so, it is difficult indeed to see how this could be possible under auspices which could remotely be called democratic. It would require an entirely new structure of parties and of mass behavior, one in which

[7] Daniel P. Moynihan, *Maximum Feasible Misunderstanding* (Glencoe, Ill.: The Free Press, 1969).

[8] Lowi, *The End of Liberalism, op. cit.,* p. 277.

Critical Elections and the Dynamics of Politics

189

political parties would be instrumentalities of democratic collective purpose. But this in turn seems inconceivable without a pre-existing revolution in social values. In the present American context such a revolution would be only too likely to be overwhelmed in its early stages by a counterrevolution among those urban and suburban whites whose values and perceived material interests would be placed in the gravest jeopardy. And who proposes to make a democratic revolution against a class which constitutes a majority of the population?

Similarly, the rise of the third party Wallace movement corresponds not only to a nationalizing of southern politics, but a southernizing of national politics. So far, at least outside the ex- Confederacy, this movement has been contained well below critical threshold levels. But it should be identified for what it is: a cryptofascist or neofascist movement dedicated to the preservation of the petit-bourgeois "little man" against the personalized conspirators—symbols for many of the large social forces at work—who are threatening both his material interests and his "way of life." That this third-party movement can be accurately described in some such terms suggests a tremendous historical change in the position and in the social values of those kinds of Americans who have been most likely in past transitional crises to support third-party insurrections against the established order.

While a detailed discussion of the etiology of fascist and extreme right-wing movements lies beyond the scope of this work, the literature on the subject emphasizes their close links with the radicalization of an anxiety-ridden middle class which is threatened with loss of either social values or social status, or both.[9] In this context, it is evident that the dominance of the middle-class individualist value system in its hitherto lib-

[9] One recent and concrete exposition of this point is William S. Allen, *The Nazi Seizure of Power* (Chicago: Quadrangle Press, 1965). See also, for example, Karl D. Bracher, *Die Auflösung der Weimarer Republik* (Villingen: Ring-Verlag, 1964), 4th ed., pp. 150–74.

eral variants presupposes, at least theoretically, its converse: that there is neither a lower nor an upper limit, granted sufficiently disruptive social conditions, to the potential appeal of a fascist movement in the United States. There are no middle-class strata locked away in a confessional party and thus immune from such mass appeals, nor is the white working class encapsulated in a Marxist class party with its collectivist vision of an alternative sociopolitical community. On the contrary, it tends to be more Bourbon than the Bourbons on many of the most divisive issues of the day.

There is no doubt that this specter has thus far in our history been nothing more than that: the very dominance of the middle-class ethic has quite precisely meant that political oppositions of European clarity and hardness, and involving social collectivities of roughly comparable size, have never had the opportunity to form in this country during the past century. Both the extreme political fragmentation of Americans and the role of the traditional parties in this system should not be discounted; they are surely limiting factors. Moreover, the role of the political entrepreneur, of inspired political leadership in an exceptionally volatile mass context where the transforming impact of leadership is maximized, cannot be overemphasized as critical to the success of any such movement.

But there may be some reason for supposing that any reorganization of our politics which involves a top-bottom coalition against a "great middle"—particularly to the extent that the polarities involve explicit challenges to the conventional Lockian wisdom of the traditional political culture—also bears within it the potential for creating "hard" oppositions. Furthermore, to the extent that changing social realities might make the transition to institutionalized domestic sovereignty necessary, the potential for a counterrevolution among the "great middle" in defense of their traditional liberties becomes not inconsiderable.

Further, the alternative of major-party absorption may be considered. The traditional process by which third-party movements have been eliminated in the past has involved absorption of some of their doctrine and most of their clienteles by one of the major parties. If this were to occur with the Wallace movement, the result might well be that the subsequent major-party alignment would pit a semisocialist (or "sovereignty-minded") party against a semifascist party, or at least one in which racism, repression of scapegoat minorities, and perhaps militarism would for the first time become a major, permanent, and activist component in its mass appeals. Finally, there is, of course, no way to determine a priori where or whether the necessary entrepreneurial skills may turn up any more than there is a priori certainty that, because emergent social tension has volatilized the mass electorate, a detonator guaranteeing realignment is sure to be ignited. All that can be said is that in an entrepreneurial political system the existence of a new and still vacant position of political leadership—one with very high potential payoff—works as a great encouragement to the emergence of such leadership.

Still, any such movement may well be blunted and diffused in its nationwide focus, not only because of the absence thus far of a nationwide explosive charge of sufficient intensity to crystallize a clear-cut countermobilization of the "great middle," but also because of the pulling apart of the several levels of the electoral-politics system by the processes of disaggregation. This continuing progression toward electoral disaggregation presupposes the disappearance at some point of system capacity for critical realignment. As this study has pointed out at some length, the critical-realignment phenomenon has been of transcendant importance in redefining the agenda and processes of American politics, though, to be sure, thus far always within a Lockian-liberal context. The disappearance of this dominant system characteristic is unthinkable except in the context of sweeping, if perhaps gradual, change in the nature of the system itself.

The evaporation of the parties as organizations relevant to the political choices of voters might indeed leave the formal structure and functioning of the electoral process largely unchanged. But this process would have lost its long-term substantive importance; the electorate would have lost what leverage it now possesses on the policy process; and it would presumably have lost as well its constituent role in the political system. It may well be that such a dissolution of party links would correspond most nearly to the continuing survival of Lockian social values in a super-developed socioeconomic system—that it would consummate a structure of politics, nearly achieved through somewhat different means in the 1920's, most functionally relevant to the basic values of middle Americans and to the most significant needs of the existing system and of the elites who manage it.

The alternatives which have been explored in the last part of this study seem at length to converge. Assuming that a revolution in values does not occur and that the patterns of change we have noted in the socioeconomic system continue to develop, the evidence would suggest that a decisive triumph of the political right is more likely than not to emerge in the near future. Like so many developments in the history of American politics, this rightist victory would most probably be a somewhat vague and ambiguous affair. It might very well emerge gradually, particularly if the trend toward electoral disaggregation continues. But if the historically progressive role of the middle class has been played out, it is only too evident that the American middle class is peculiarly subject to threat and anxiety as a fruit both of the international and domestic transformations which have unfolded since World War II.

What kind of right would triumph? The answer to this question can be provided only when it is known whether the "great middle" is becoming revolutionized politically under the overwhelming pressure of sharp blows. If this happens, the result may well be the emergence of even stronger extreme-right, racist, and perhaps militarist movements in our electoral politics than any which have appeared during this decade. This would be particularly likely in the event that economic disruption, steeply increasing the costs of middle-class flight to the suburbs and generating zero-sum conflict between blue-collar whites and blacks, should occur. Our next, and perhaps last, critical realignment would almost certainly follow. If, as seems more probable, no adequate nationwide stimulus emerges which might radicalize the "great middle," the most likely outcome would be the development of an *Obrigkeitsstaat*—perhaps somewhat analogous to the German regime under Wilhelm II—in which the executive establishment exercises an unchallenged, unfettered ascendancy in policy-making. We have come a long distance along this road since World War II, particularly in the areas of foreign policy and war-making: the attitudes of successive presidents during the 1960's toward their responsibilities in the conduct of the Vietnam war indicate a conception of role, and of responsibilities to domestic clienteles, which has a distinctly Hohenzollern flavor.

Whatever the outcome may be, the crisis of our time is at bottom the crisis of traditional Lockian ideology and institutions in an age marked by their increasingly obvious irrelevance to the policy choices at hand. The Chinese have a proverbial curse: "May you live in interesting times." We surely do; and whatever the course of our history as we pass through the greatest of our transitional crises may be, the American political system is not likely to emerge unchanged from its ordeal.

Appendix

Transformations in the Shapes of Electoral Politics in Five States: 1880-1968

Table 1 Indiana: 1880–1968

Year	Mean % Democratic of 2-Party Vote	Variance	Standard Deviation	Rolloff	Turnout	Dropoff
1880	49.4	0.00	0.07	0.1	94.5	
1882	51.2	*			85.9	5.6
1884	50.8	0.01	0.10	0.6	90.2	
1886	49.5	0.04	0.21	0.2	85.3	4.1
1888	49.8	0.00	0.05	0.3	93.3	
1890	52.2	0.03	0.18	1.1	80.3	11.0
1892	50.7	0.00	0.03	1.1	89.4	
1894	45.6	0.01	0.09	1.9	87.2	+1.5
1896	48.1	0.08	0.28	2.6	95.2	
1898	48.3	0.01	0.09	1.9	82.5	10.0
1900	48.0	0.00	0.05	1.4	92.2	
1902	46.9	0.24	0.49	2.8	79.6	11.2
1904	43.1	0.03	0.17	3.3	89.6	
1906	47.1	0.00	0.05	1.5	75.4	13.6
1908	50.0	0.21	0.46	2.0	89.9	
1910	51.1	0.00	0.05	1.9	76.2	13.0
1912	47.5	0.02	0.14	2.7	77.8	

Table 1   Indiana: 1880–1968 (*Continued*)

Year	Mean % Democratic of 2-Party Vote	Variance	Standard Deviation	Rolloff	Turnout	Dropoff
(3-party)						
1914	45.2	0.11	0.33	3.6	75.2	1.3
(3-party)						
1916	49.1	0.03	0.16	2.2	81.9	
1918	45.5	0.01	0.08	1.9	63.9	20.3
1920	43.0	0.21	0.46	3.2	70.9	
1922	50.2	2.39	1.55	3.2	61.2	15.1
1924	45.8	5.10	2.26	4.7	70.7	
1926	48.0	1.01	1.00	3.1	56.5	17.9
1928	44.1	4.69	2.17	1.6	74.9	
1930	52.0	0.03	0.17	2.0	62.5	14.4
1932	56.3	0.05	0.22	1.2	79.0	
1934	51.8	0.02	0.15	2.4	72.1	6.5
1936	56.3	0.34	0.58	2.8	78.7	
1938	50.2	0.02	0.13	1.9	73.6	4.2
1940	49.7	0.07	0.26	1.5	81.1	
1942	45.2	0.01	0.10	1.0	56.9	27.7
1944	47.9	0.39	0.62	2.3	71.7	
1946	43.6	0.10	0.32	1.6	56.1	19.5
1948	51.9	1.26	1.12	2.1	67.2	
1950	46.3	0.08	0.28	1.4	63.1	3.5
1952	44.0	1.99	1.41	1.9	75.8	
1954	48.8	0.07	0.27	0.8	60.5	18.7
1956	43.8	2.04	1.43	2.2	73.7	
1958	55.6	0.33	0.58	1.0	62.7	13.4
1960	49.1	1.82	1.35	1.5	76.9	
1962	49.9	0.16	0.40	2.0	63.9	15.7
1964	54.8	0.43	0.66	3.4	73.1	
1966	46.2	0.06	0.25	2.0	57.4	20.4
1968	46.2	3.13	1.77	6.8	72.2	

* Secretary of State only.

Table 2 Massachusetts: 1880–1966

Year	Mean % Democratic of 2-Party Vote	Variance	Standard Deviation	Rolloff	Turnout	Dropoff
1880	40.1	0.03	0.18	0.4	71.2	
1881	35.9	0.03	0.17	3.4	38.7	54.4
1882	46.7	7.61	2.76	1.1	61.3	13.9
1883	47.2	0.43	0.66	0.2	72.9	+2.4
1884	41.1	3.40	1.84	1.9	69.3	
1885	44.7	0.25	0.50	1.5	46.7	32.6
1886	48.0	0.29	0.54	0.3	53.0	23.5
1887	45.5	0.26	0.51	0.1	56.6	18.3
1888	44.8	0.25	0.50	0.4	71.7	
1889 *	45.6	2.16	1.47	5.2	53.6	25.2
1890	49.6	2.23	1.49	5.3	56.9	20.6
1891	48.3	1.52	1.24	5.0	62.7	12.6
1892	47.3	2.20	1.48	10.2	74.6	
1893	43.5	0.57	0.75	3.8	68.1	8.7
1894	38.8	0.67	0.82	3.8	61.3	17.8
1895	39.0	0.16	0.40	4.0	58.7	21.3
1896	25.5	6.95	2.64	11.4	70.6	
1897	35.9	0.32	0.57	5.9	46.4	34.3
1898	36.3	0.17	0.41	5.9	53.0	24.9
1899	37.0	0.47	0.68	4.6	49.5	29.9
1900	36.5	2.97	1.72	14.7	67.4	
1901	37.6	0.39	0.62	7.0	51.8	23.1
1902	41.5	2.54	1.59	7.5	62.6	7.1
1903	41.9	2.78	1.67	9.1	61.2	9.2
1904	43.1	23.95	4.89	12.6	67.6	
1905	43.0	18.62	4.32	7.8	58.5	13.5
1906	43.5	12.50	3.54	9.8	63.4	6.2
1907	31.2	1.41	1.19	9.8	41.4	39.2
1908	36.9	7.28	2.70	14.0	65.1	
1909	44.0	14.65	3.83	8.5	54.5	16.3
1910	48.3	9.32	3.05	8.5	61.0	6.3
1911	47.3	4.81	2.19	8.4	58.9	9.5
1912 (3-party)	39.5	5.00	2.24	8.8	63.4	
1913 (3-party)	41.8	0.98	0.99	7.8	58.3	8.0

Table 2   Massachusetts: 1880–1966 (*Continued*)

Year	Mean % Democratic of 2-Party Vote	Variance	Standard Deviation	Rolloff	Turnout	Dropoff
1914 (3-party)	45.3	1.53	1.24	5.8	56.6	10.7
1915	43.5	7.56	2.74	6.8	60.5	4.6
1916	42.7	10.99	3.31	10.0	62.8	
1917	37.1	1.01	1.01	6.8	44.1	29.8
1918	44.0	14.92	3.86	5.2	47.7	23.0
1919	38.2	3.83	1.97	7.5	55.8	11.1
1920	30.3	5.24	2.29	9.3	53.3	
1922	43.5	12.80	3.58	9.2	46.1	13.5
1924	39.6	44.36	6.66	12.5	56.6	
1926	44.1	21.25	4.61	12.1	48.6	14.1
1928	48.9	6.15	2.48	9.5	74.0	
1930	51.1	16.58	4.07	6.4	55.7	24.7
1932	51.7	3.27	1.81	6.2	69.5	
1934	54.4	12.52	3.54	5.6	63.2	9.1
1936	50.3	8.75	2.96	5.6	74.2	
1938	46.4	19.41	4.41	3.9	70.6	4.8
1940	50.1	11.67	3.42	6.1	78.7	
1942	47.4	7.73	2.78	5.1	52.5	33.3
1944	50.8	21.76	4.67	4.7	71.0	
1946	45.5	13.83	3.72	3.5	59.0	16.9
1948	55.2	21.32	4.62	4.4	71.5	
1950	56.4	10.43	3.23	4.3	62.9	12.0
1952	49.2	12.81	3.58	5.1	75.0	
1954	51.9	18.88	4.34	3.8	59.1	21.2
1956	51.3	25.24	5.02	4.8	72.0	
1958	61.8	36.10	6.01	4.3	57.5	20.1
1960	55.3	42.40	6.51	6.8	73.8	
1962	56.6	63.11	7.94	6.1	63.2	14.4
1964	59.7	201.81	14.21	8.7	70.3	
1966	51.5	139.03	11.79	6.2	61.3	12.8

* Australian ballot (office-block format) introduced effective with 1889 election.

Table 3 Michigan: 1880–1966

Year	Mean % Democratic of 2-Party Vote	Variance	Standard Deviation	Rolloff	Turnout	Dropoff
1880	41.9	0.60	0.77	1.8	75.5	
1882	48.7	0.63	0.82	0.4	62.7	17.0
1884	49.4	0.01	0.09	2.6	76.0	
1886	48.7	0.18	0.42	0.2	68.3	10.1
1888	47.6	0.05	0.21	0.2	80.9	
1890	50.7	0.55	0.74	0.2	64.4	20.4
1892	48.1	1.17	1.08	4.7	73.2	
1894	35.4	3.14	1.77	3.2	76.8	+4.9
1896	44.2	0.61	0.78	1.1	95.3	
1898	41.8	0.22	0.47	1.3	71.0	25.5
1900	40.6	0.55	0.74	0.8	89.0	
1902	41.0	2.96	1.72	1.1	63.3	28.9
1904	32.8	18.60	4.32	2.2	78.9	
1906	34.9	0.42	0.64	2.4	54.6	30.8
1908	36.9	21.25	4.61	1.1	75.9	
1910	38.4	6.40	2.53	2.7	52.3	31.1
1912 (3-party)	31.0	7.04	2.65	0.9	69.8	
1914 (3-party)	42.3	38.06	6.17	4.5	52.7	24.5
1916	42.5	1.65	1.28	1.4	72.9	
1918	37.6	27.02	5.20	5.0	46.3	36.5
1920	24.9	6.58	2.56	2.1	55.1	
1922	36.5	45.26	6.73	7.0	28.9	47.5
1924	20.6	27.21	5.22	6.4	53.7	
1926	28.1	13.65	3.70	9.6	27.4	49.0
1928	28.2	0.66	0.81	2.6	56.3	
1930	30.3	41.86	6.47	12.5	33.0	41.4
1932	52.1	4.12	2.03	7.6	62.0	
1934	48.9	2.31	1.52	6.3	45.0	27.4
1936	54.0	6.45	2.54	8.8	62.1	
1938	47.5	1.34	1.16	5.8	53.1	14.5
1940	49.0	5.71	2.39	6.7	66.6	
1942	45.6	5.05	2.25	8.3	31.2	44.1
1944	46.7	3.33	1.82	3.3	63.7	

Table 3 Michigan: 1880–1966 (*Continued*)

Year	Mean % Democratic of 2-Party Vote	Variance	Standard Deviation	Rolloff	Turnout	Dropoff
1946	36.9	4.35	2.09	6.4	45.9	27.9
1948	50.01	2.62	1.62	3.6	55.6	
1950	47.1	2.94	1.71	5.8	47.4	14.7
1952	47.6	2.82	1.68	3.3	68.5	
1954	52.4	3.07	1.75	3.5	51.0	25.5
1956	50.8	9.22	3.04	3.6	71.1	
1958	54.4	1.62	1.27	3.7	51.9	27.0
1960	52.1	1.68	1.30	4.2	72.4	
1962	51.4	5.89	2.43	4.7	59.2	18.2
1964	59.6	83.89	9.16	5.1	67.3	
1966	48.1	61.84	7.86	5.3	50.8	24.5

Table 4 Rhode Island: 1880–1966

Year	Mean % Democratic of 2-Party Vote *	Variance	Standard Deviation	Rolloff	Turnout	Dropoff
1880	34.9	14.89	3.86	1.8	37.8	
1881	31.4	0.40	0.63	1.8	26.1	31.0
1882	35.2	3.79	1.95	1.7	24.2	35.0
1883	43.3	0.42	0.65	0.7	36.3	4.0
1884	37.5	0.03	0.18	0.8	37.5	
1885	40.7	0.48	0.69	1.9	31.8	15.2
1886	43.2	24.70	4.97	1.1	37.2	0.8
1887	53.2	1.17	1.08	2.0	47.3	+26.1
1888	46.0	0.24	0.49	0.9	51.8	
1889 **	56.8 (Governor only)				55.0	+6.2
1890	50.5	0.23	0.48	4.2	52.4	+1.2
1891	50.4	0.80	0.89	3.5	55.2	+6.6
1892	48.0	0.32	0.57	2.3	64.7	
1893	49.8	0.95	0.97	2.4	54.4	15.9
1894	43.7 (Governor only)				62.0	4.1
1895	36.1	0.45	0.67	2.0	48.7	24.7
1896	37.6	0.24	0.49	1.9	54.5	

Year	Mean % Democratic of 2-Party Vote	Variance	Standard Deviation	Rolloff	Turnout	Dropoff
1897	35.4	1.60	1.27	3.9	44.2	18.9
1898	35.4	2.43	1.56	7.3	44.3	18.7
1899	37.2	1.42	1.19	5.7	43.8	19.6
1900	38.8	1.56	1.25	2.8	47.6	
1901	39.9	2.75	1.66	2.4	46.5	2.3
1902	50.7	12.24	3.50	2.5	57.2	+20.2
1903	47.6	7.74	2.78	2.2	58.3	+22.5
1904	43.8	15.55	3.94	2.1	63.8	
1905	42.6	3.01	1.73	3.2	53.3	16.5
1906	47.5	5.78	2.40	2.8	59.4	6.9
1907	47.8	8.68	2.95	3.6	58.0	9.1
1908	39.9	10.30	1.10	5.8	63.5	
1909	39.9	1.72	1.31	3.9	55.3	12.9
1910	45.2	8.79	2.96	2.5	56.5	11.0
1911	43.6	2.13	1.46	4.1	58.4	8.0
1912 (3-party)	41.1	26.59	5.16	11.3	62.7	
1914 (3-party)	40.4	6.81	2.61	2.8	60.7	3.2
1916	44.8	22.35	4.73	2.3	65.8	
1918	44.6	2.51	1.59	3.2	58.2	11.6
1920	34.2	0.30	0.55	2.8	57.9	
1922	51.6	3.14	1.77	1.8	52.2	9.8
1924	41.2	2.57	1.60	1.2	66.3	
1926	42.9	3.11	1.76	1.8	53.5	19.3
1928	48.8	0.59	0.76	1.1	68.9	
1930	49.1	0.17	0.41	1.5	62.0	10.0
1932	55.3	0.35	0.59	1.0	71.7	
1934	57.4	0.11	0.34	1.0	64.4	10.2
1936	53.9	4.07	2.02	3.4	78.0	
1938	45.9	1.32	1.15	2.4	75.7	2.9
1940	55.6	0.34	0.58	2.4	75.6	
1942	58.2	0.11	0.33	1.4	53.8	29.0
1944	59.7	0.97	0.99	1.7	65.0	
1946	54.5	0.21	0.45	2.3	57.6	11.4
1948	60.0	0.91	0.95	4.0	66.0	

Table 4   Rhode Island: 1880–1966 (*Continued*)

Year	Mean % Democratic of 2-Party Vote	Variance	Standard Deviation	Rolloff	Turnout	Dropoff
1950	60.9	0.74	0.86	2.2	57.7	12.6
1952	52.8	2.71	1.65	2.7	79.8	
1954	59.1	0.45	0.67	1.9	62.7	21.4
1956	49.7	13.12	3.62	3.8	73.2	
1958	56.1	21.26	4.61	3.7	64.9	11.3
1960	62.3	13.17	3.63	4.5	75.1	
1962	56.8	14.22	3.77	4.3	60.6	19.3
1964	63.2	209.01	14.46	8.4	72.0	
1966	49.9	91.57	9.57	6.6	61.2	15.0
1968	55.6	41.03	6.41	6.9	70.9	

* State elections from 1880 through 1911 were held annually in April; no presidential elections are included in the means until 1912.

** Rhode Island freehold property qualifications for voting were abolished effective with the 1889 state election; the party-column type of Australian ballot was introduced prior to the 1890 election.

Table 5   Wisconsin: 1881–1968

Year	Mean % Democratic of Total Vote	Variance	Standard Deviation	Rolloff	Turnout	Dropoff
1881	45.3	0.37	0.61	3.0	71.0	
1884	44.6	5.31	2.30	0.6	82.2	
1886	40.7	0.37	0.61	0.8	69.3	15.7
1888	43.7	0.02	0.12	0.1	81.1	
1890	52.4	0.08	0.29	2.5	67.0	17.4
1892	47.9	0.01	0.09	0.7	76.8	
1894	37.2	0.10	0.32	1.5	74.3	3.3
1896	37.8	0.09	0.30	1.1	84.9	
1898	38.9	0.85	0.92	1.4	60.0	29.4
1900	36.3	0.02	0.13	0.6	77.5	
1902	38.4	0.77	0.87	6.8	61.6	20.5
1904	34.1	9.72	3.12	6.8	72.0	
1906	32.4	0.24	0.48	3.1	50.1	30.5

Year	Mean % Democratic of 2-Party Vote	Variance	Standard Deviation	Rolloff	Turnout	Dropoff
1908	36.0	0.34	0.58	3.0	68.7	
1910	34.0	0.13	0.36	4.0	57.6	16.2
1912	42.0	4.31	2.08	5.9	68.7	
1914	38.6	6.94	2.64	7.0	53.3	22.5
1916	35.4	14.68	3.83	8.2	70.2	
1918	28.6	10.94	3.31	4.3	49.2	29.9
1920	17.1	56.56	7.52	18.8	52.3	
1922	11.1	7.77	2.79	14.1	34.2	34.6
1924	24.3	107.70	10.38	15.5	57.3	
1926	11.0	11.72	3.42	17.6	36.1	37.0
1928	32.1	64.96	8.06	27.0	65.9	
1930	23.3	7.28	2.70	12.9	36.6	44.5
1932	52.3	43.59	6.60	7.7	65.1	
1934	32.7	29.94	5.47	9.3	53.9	17.2
1936	33.0	251.94	15.87	13.3	68.9	
1938	14.4	32.78	5.73	8.5	52.1	24.4
1940	23.3	147.93	12.16	12.3	72.4	
1942	15.5	5.91	2.43	9.8	40.2	44.5
1944	39.9	22.70	4.77	9.3	65.7	
1946	34.1	20.09	4.48	6.2	49.9	24.0
1948	46.7	17.82	4.22	5.6	59.8	
1950	42.5	13.78	3.71	3.3	52.1	12.9
1952	37.7	14.17	3.76	4.8	72.5	
1954	45.6	4.65	2.16	3.6	51.4	29.1
1956	42.7	11.26	3.36	7.9	67.8	
1958	52.3	9.29	3.05	5.1	51.8	23.6
1960	48.7	6.53	2.56	4.5	73.4	
1962	48.1	11.01	3.32	4.5	53.2	27.5
1964	52.1	28.59	5.35	4.7	70.3	
1966	46.6	27.95	5.29	4.0	48.1	31.6
1968	45.8	57.47	7.58	7.2	68.8	

Index